Study Guide

To Accompany

Families in Context

Study Guide

To Accompany

Families in Context

Second Edition

Gene H. Starbuck

Paradigm Publishers
Boulder • London

Copyright © 2006 Paradigm Publishers

Published in the United States by Paradigm Publishers, 3360 Mitchell Lane Suite E, Boulder, CO 80301 USA.

Paradigm Publishers is the trade name of Birkenkamp & Company, LLC, Dean Birkenkamp, President and Publisher.

Library of Congress Cataloging-in-Publication Data
Starbuck, Gene H.
  Study guide to accompany Families in context / Gene H. Starbuck.—2nd ed.
      p. cm.
  ISBN-13: 978-1-59451-199-8 (pb)
  ISBN-10: 1-59451-199-3 (pb)
  1. Family—Examinations, questions, etc. 2. Family—Problems, exercises, etc. 3. Family—United States—Examinations, questions, etc. 4. Family—United states—Problems, exercises, etc. I. Starbuck, Gene H.
Families in context. II. Title.
  HQ728.S79 2006b
  306.85076--dc22

                                                                              2006012894

Printed and bound in the United States of America on acid free paper that meets the standards of the American National Standard for Permanence of Paper for Printed Library Materials.

10 09 08 07 06   1 2 3 4 5

Contents

Preface

This Study Guide is designed to help students review and apply the material presented in the textbook, *Families in Context*. Many of the sample questions were originally prepared by Wanda Clark for the first edition of the textbook. The organization of this study guide corresponds to chapters in *Families in Context*. Each chapter contains the following elements:

Learning Objectives

Learning objectives provide a brief list of the major points that students should gather from their study of the chapter.

Chapter Outline

The "Thinking Ahead" and "Rethinking in Context" questions from the text are reproduced here. Chapter outlines offer an overview of the structure and emphasis of the chapter. Students might want to read the Learning Objectives and Chapter Outline before actually reading the textbook chapter.

Multiple Choice Questions, True/False Questions, Matching Question

Students can use these to test their mastery of the material. They should probably ask the instructor whether any of these questions will be on the actual test.

Short Essay, Critical Thinking, and Group Discussion Exercises

The essay and critical thinking exercises help develop writing, organizational, and analytical ability. The short essay questions can be answered with reference to material in the textbook. The critical thinking questions often require reference to outside sources such as Internet sites. Group discussion exercises are designed for discussion by students in small groups that might be arranged by the course instructor.

Answer Key

The answer key includes correct responses to objective questions and outlines the major points of the short essay questions.

Survey of Opinions and Experiences

The study guide concludes with a questionnaire about attitudes and experiences related to the family. Even if your instructor does not ask you to complete the questionnaire, you might look it over anyway. It will give you an idea about how survey questions are sometimes constructed. Most of these questions are from the General Social Survey, which provides much of the data reported in the text.

Chapter 1 Defining Family Variation

Learning Objectives

After reading this chapter, you should be able to
1. Understand the complexities of defining "family" and be able to describe various family forms.
2. Discuss the criteria for constructing definitions of family, including values and norms.
3. Outline the differences between structural and functional as well as macro and micro definitions of family.
4. Comprehend the case studies of Nayar and Israeli Kibbutz families as examples of alternative family forms.
5. Describe and apply Weber's concept of "ideal type" to family systems.
6. Discuss gender in families as it relates to authority, power, inheritance, and residence.
7. Apply Money's typology of gender roles.
8. Explain both pessimistic and optimistic outlooks for the "family decline" debate.

Chapter Outline

Thinking Ahead: Write a definition of the family. Make sure that your definition includes all those groups of persons you think of as being a family, while ruling out all groups that you think do not constitute a family.

1) Basic Considerations
    a)   What is family?
        i)   Nuclear
        ii)   Conjugal unit
        iii) Extended family
        iv) Family of orientation
        v)   Family of procreation
        vi) Stepfamily
        vii) Household

2) Criteria for Judgments
    a)   Values
    b)   Norms
        i)   Informal norms
        ii)   Formal norms
        iii) Roles and scripts
    c)   Types of definitions
        i)   Functional definitions
             (1) Microfunctional
             (2) Macrofunctional
        ii)   Structural definitions

   d) Defining marriage
   e) Alternative families elsewhere
       i)   Nayar
       ii) Israeli kibbutz

3) Ideal Types, Dichotomies and Continua

4) Gender
   a) Authority
   b) Descent and inheritance
   c) Residence patterns
   d) Gender role continuum
   e) Types of gender roles
       i)   Sex-irreducible gender roles
       ii)   Sex-influenced gender roles
       iii) Sex-arbitrary gender roles

5) The "Family Decline" Debate
   a) The pessimistic position
   b) The optimistic position
       i)   Glad it changed optimists
       ii) Did not really change optimists

Rethinking in Context: Reconsider your initial definition of the family. Did it include all groups you had in mind? Did it exclude groups you do not think of as families? What values and norms are reflected in your definition? Was your definition more functional or more structural?

Ask five acquaintances to tell you about their families. What roles do they identify as part of their families? What kind of families did they describe?

Where do you stand on the family-decline debate? Why? What additional information would you need to be sure you are right?

Multiple Choice Questions

   1.   Susan and Trent are married to each other but have no children. They may be considered a(n)
        a. Extended family
        b. Conjugal unit
        c. Nuclear family
        d. Family of procreation

2.   James lives with his biological father and his sister and brother. This is referred to as his
     a.   Family of procreation
     b.   Family of orientation
     c.   Stepfamily
     d.   Extended family

3.   Kate and Liz have been partners for ten years and recently they adopted a child. Kate and Liz would call this their
     a.   Family of orientation
     b.   Extended family
     c.   Family of procreation
     d.   Blended family

4.   Joe has divorced his wife and refuses to pay the child support that was ordered for their three children. Joe has violated
     a.   The principle of pronatalism
     b.   An informal norm
     c.   A formal norm
     d.   A neolocal assumption

5.   Juan and Maria have one child. Their extended family members keep asking when they are planning to have another. This illustrates
     a.   A formal norm
     b.   Blasphemy
     c.   Pronuptialism
     d.   Pronatalism

6.   Even before they got married, John and Priscilla had learned a great deal about how a husband and wife generally interact with each other in their society. They have learned the marital _____.
     a.   Role
     b.   Script
     c.   Dance
     d.   Dissonance

7.   Anthony and Ben are members of a fraternity at college and live in the fraternity house with several of their fraternity brothers. Which of the following types of definitions would be most likely to refer to this as a family?
     a.   Institutional
     b.   Macrofunctional
     c.   Microfunctional
     d.   Structural

8. According to the U.S. Census Bureau definition of a family, members must
    a. Be related by blood, marriage, or adoption
    b. Share the same residence
    c. Both (a) and (b) above
    d. None of the above

9. Tom lives next door to a person he calls "Uncle Ralph" even though they are not related by blood. Uncle Ralph would be called
    a. Extended family
    b. Fictive kin
    c. Stepfamily
    d. Dysfunctional family

10. Rodney and Gene consider themselves married even though they cannot legally marry as a gay couple. They would be considered _____ but not _____.
    a. Legally wed; functionally wed
    b. Functionally wed; legally wed
    c. Fictive kin; extended family
    d. Structurally partners; functionally wed

11. Some of the marriage benefits not afforded currently to gay and lesbian couples, in most states, include
    a. Health benefits
    b. Bereavement leave
    c. Inheritance rights
    d. All of the above

12. One of the criteria for forming a "common law" marriage is
    a. Intent
    b. Shared finances
    c. Living in the same household
    d. Having a child together

13. The Nayar example illustrates
    a. Multiple definitions of the role of "father"
    b. A matriarchal society
    c. A society without kinship terms
    d. An androgynous society

14. The example of the Israeli Kibbutz demonstrates
    a. Kinships based on community values and structures
    b. Parents who did not care about children
    c. A rigidly divided gender role system
    d. Antinuptualism

15. A woman taking her husband's name when they marry could be considered an example of
    a. matrilineal descent
    b. patrilocal residence
    c. patrilineal descent
    d. matrilocal residence

16. The most common residence pattern for newly married couples in the United States is
    a. Matrilocal
    b. Patrilocal
    c. Neolocal
    d. Avunculocal

17. The person who developed a typology of gender roles was
    a. Max Weber
    b. Karl Marx
    c. John Money
    d. Gloria Steinem

18. Susan has just given birth to her first child and is breastfeeding. This is a example of a(n)
    a. Sex-influenced gender role
    b. Sex-irreducible gender role
    c. Sex-arbitrary gender role
    d. Androgynous gender role

19. Scholars who are concerned about the "defathering" of the family institution represent
    a. The pessimistic viewpoint on the family decline debate
    b. The "glad it changed" viewpoint on the family decline debate
    c. The "it hasn't really changed" viewpoint on the family decline debate
    d. Theorists who aren't interested in the family

20. Proponents of the optimist side of the "family decline" debate would be likely to encourage discussions of
    a. Family diversity
    b. Gender role changes
    c. Power structures in family and society
    d. All of the above

True/False

1. An extended family often includes grandparents.
2. A family that includes children from both parents who have divorced can be called a complex stepfamily, a blended family, or a reconstituted family.
3. The most frequent type of household in the year 2000 was married couples with children.
4. Families are portrayed by TV sitcoms today much as they were in the 1950s and 1960s.
5. The type of household most likely to decrease by 2010 is men living alone.
6. "Traditional family values" is a perspective often based on a Judeo-Christian religious tradition.
7. A prescriptive norm determines what should not be done.
8. A "POSSLQ" means a person of suspicious sexual and licentious qualities.
9. Incest taboos are not found in all societies.
10. When using a legal definition of marriage, divorce is necessary to end the relationship.

Matching

The terms introduced in this chapter are listed here in alphabetical order. Match the terms with the appropriate definition.

_____	1	Androgyny	A	(1)(Legalistic definition): The legal union of a man and woman as husband and wife. (2)A socially sanctioned sexual and economic union between two (or more) members of opposite sexes (occasionally between members of the same sex). (3) A socially approved sexual union of some permanence between two or more individuals.
_____	2	Authority	B	(1) A system of norms, values, statuses, and roles that develop around a basic social goal; (2) A regular and traditional way of meeting a society's needs.
_____	3	Bilateral	C	(1) Divided into two parts. (2) The division of a continuum into two mutually exclusive parts.
_____	4	Common-Law Marriage	D	A belief system that encourages childbearing.
_____	5	Conjugal unit	E	A belief system that encourages marriage
_____	6	Continuum	F	A custom that newlyweds are expected to live separately from either's family.
_____	7	Dichotomy	G	A custom that newlyweds are expected to live with the bride's relatives.
_____	8	Extended family	H	A custom that newlyweds are expected to live with the groom's relatives.
_____	9	Familism	I	A family composed of the nuclear family plus additional relatives, usually a third generation.

____	10	Family of orientation	J	A family in which the mother-child bond takes precedence over the husband-wife bond and in which the day-to-day problems of family living (especially child care and socialization) are managed by women.
____	11	Family of procreation	K	A hypothetical construct used for comparisons.
____	12	Fictive kin	L	A living unit; a group of persons sharing living quarters.
____	13	Formal norms	M	A position in the social system.
____	14	Functional definition	N	A public ceremony in recognition of a change in status.
____	15	Gender	O	A rule forbidding marriage or sexual activity among closely related persons.
____	16	Household	P	A social condition in which there is no gender role differentiation.
____	17	Ideal type	Q	A system in which men have the authority.
____	18	Incest taboo	R	A system in which women have the authority.
____	19	Informal norms	S	A two-generation group that includes parents and their children.
____	20	Institution	T	A union legally recognized as a marriage in spite of not having been solemnized by the state.
____	21	Kin group	U	Basic differences in expectations that define the differences between men and women.
____	22	Macrofunctional	V	Behavioral expectations that are written and enforced by specialized social mechanisms; laws.
____	23	Marriage	W	Behavioral expectations that lack codified, enforceable sanctions.
____	24	Matriarchy	X	Definition based on how the family serves the participating individuals or how it serves society.
____	25	Matrifocal family	Y	Definition describing the components and makeup of a family.
____	26	Matrilineal	Z	Expectation influenced, but not fully determined, by secondary sex characteristics and other biological differences of men and women.
____	27	Matrilocal residence	AA	Expectations associated with a particular position in the social system.
____	28	Microfunctional	AB	Expectations governing the interaction of two or more roles.
____	29	Neolocal residence	AC	Expectations that could as easily be the opposite.
____	30	Norm	AD	Family unit consisting of a married man and woman, plus children from a previous relationship.
____	31	Nuclear family	AE	Focusing on consequences for individuals or small groups.

____	32	Patriarchy	AF	Focusing on consequences for institutions or societies.
____	33	Patrilineal	AG	Network of persons related by blood, marriage, or adoption.
____	34	Patrilocal residence	AH	Persons treated as if they are related.
____	35	Power	AI	Shared ideas about what is good, right, or proper.
____	36	Pronatalism	AJ	The actual ability to exercise one's will over others.
____	37	Pronuptialism	AK	The belief in a strong sense of family identification and loyalty, mutual assistance among family members, a concern for the perpetuation of the family unit, and the subordination of the interests and personality of individual family members to the interests and welfare of the family group.
____	38	Rite of passage	AL	The biological fact of being female or male.
____	39	Role	AM	The family unit that includes one's parents and siblings.
____	40	Script	AN	The family unit that includes one's spouse and, at least potentially, one's children.
____	41	Sex	AO	The husband-wife pair.
____	42	Sex-arbitrary gender roles	AP	The social fact of being feminine or masculine.
____	43	Sex-influenced gender roles	AQ	The socially granted right to control and influence others.
____	44	Sex-Irreducible gender roles	AR	Tracing descent and inheritance through both male and female lines.
____	45	Status	AS	Tracing descent and inheritance through female lines.
____	46	Stepfamily	AT	Tracing descent and inheritance through male lines.
____	47	Structural definition	AU	Unbroken degrees of measurement between two extremes.
____	48	Values	AV	Widespread expectations governing behavior.

Short Essay

1. Defining "family" is difficult for several reasons. Discuss at least two of the factors that make this a complex task.
2. Discuss at least two of the normative expectations associated with traditional marriage.
3. Using John Money's typology of gender roles, define and provide an example of each of the three possible role types.

Critical Thinking

1. In Utah, some people continue to violate state law and the position of the Mormon Church by practicing polygamy. Many cultures around the world also see polygamy as acceptable. If you were responsible for setting policy on polygamy, how would you proceed? On what would you base your decisions? How would you research this phenomenon?
2. Select a recent TV sitcom or drama show that illustrates a particular family form other than a nuclear family. Discuss, using concrete examples, how or whether this show has contributed to stereotyping of that particular family form.
3. Where do you stand on the "family decline" debate? What kinds of evidence would support your position? What kinds of evidence might oppose your position? How would you counter the latter evidence to support your position?

Additional Small Group Discussion

As a group, write a definition of family that you can all agree on. What groups that you might not consider to be a family would be included under that definition? What groups might be left out? What personal values become apparent in the construction of the definition? What norms are indicated? Would this be a satisfactory definition if you were responsible for counting the number of families in your community?

Answer Keys

Multiple Choice

1.	b	6.	b	11.	d	16.	c
2.	b	7.	c	12.	a	17.	c
3.	c	8.	c	13.	a	18.	b
4.	c	9.	b	14.	a	19.	a
5.	d	10.	b	15.	c	20.	d

True/False

1.	t	6.	t
2.	t	7.	f
3.	f	8.	f
4.	f	9.	f
5.	f	10.	t

Matching

1.	P	11.	AN	21.	AG	31.	S	41.	AL
2.	AQ	12.	AH	22.	AF	32.	Q	42.	AC
3.	AR	13.	V	23.	A	33.	AT	43.	Z
4.	T	14.	X	24.	R	34.	H	44.	U
5.	AO	15.	AP	25.	J	35.	AJ	45.	M
6.	AU	16.	L	26.	AS	36.	D	46.	AD
7.	C	17.	K	27.	G	37.	E	47.	Y
8.	I	18.	O	28.	AE	38.	N	48.	AI
9.	AK	19.	W	29.	F	39.	AA		
10.	AM	20.	B	30.	AV	40.	AB		

Short Essay

1. Defining "family" is difficult for several reasons. Discuss at least two of the factors that make this a complex task.
   a. Values (traditional vs. nontraditional)
   b. Purpose of definition
   c. Types of norms (informal and formal)
   d. Roles and scripts
   e. Types of definitions (functional vs. structural)

2. Discuss at least two of the normative expectations associated with traditional marriage.
   a. Premarital sex
   b. "Living in sin"
   c. Economic cooperation
   d. Rights to inheritance
   e. Pronatalism

3. Using John Money's typology of gender roles, define and provide an example of each of the three possible role types.
   a. Sex-irreducible: men impregnate, women gestate and lactate
   b. Sex-influenced: several possibilities
   c. Sex-arbitrary: several possibilities

Chapter 2 Studying the Family

Learning Objectives

After reading this chapter, you should be able to
1. Provide working definitions of sociology.
2. Distinguish between sociology as a science using quantitative methodologies and as a humanistic analysis using qualitative methodologies.
3. Describe the goals of scientific study.
4. Explain the differences between value free and value aware research.
5. Discuss the advantages and disadvantages of specific methods such as controlled experiments, survey research, field research, unobtrusive research, and program evaluation.
6. Explain the importance of regularities to social scientists.
7. Locate each macro-sociological theory within its historical context and explain major tenets and critiques of functionalism, conflict/feminist theories, and ecological evolutionary approaches.
8. Contrast microsociological perspectives with macro theories.
9. Outline major tenets of each microsociological theory such as symbolic interactionism; compare with social exchange theory, developmental perspectives, and family systems theory.
10. Describe how the scripting model is a synthesis between macro and micro approaches.

Chapter Outline

Thinking Ahead: Based on what you have learned from this book or elsewhere, make up a definition of "sociology." What do sociologists study? What methods do they use to gather their information? How do you expect a college-level social science course about the family to be different from more popular sources of information such as television talk shows?

1) What Is Sociology?
   a) Sociology as science
      i) Objectivity
      ii) Replication
      iii) Testability
      iv) Precision of definition and measurement
      v) Positivist approach
   b) Sociology as humanistic studies
      i) Post-positivist approach
      ii) Value aware
   c) Other fields in family studies
      i) Psychology
      ii) Anthropology

6) Micro-Macro Synthesis: The Scripting Model
   a)   Societal scripts
   b)   Personal scripts
   c)   Scenes
   d)   Mutual scripts

Rethinking in Context: Consider your Thinking Forward answers. Would you change any of them now that you have read this chapter? Why or why not? Of conflict theory, functionalism, and symbolic interactionism, which provides a better explanation for gender-role differences?

Multiple Choice Questions

1.   Which of the following is least likely to be part of a definition of sociology?
     a.   Scientific study using specific research methods
     b.   Studies institutions
     c.   Studies groups
     d.   Studies individuals

2. Which of the following is not a criterion for scientific study?
     a.   Replication
     b.   Testability
     c.   Subjectivity
     d.   Precision of definition and measurement

3.   Which of the following disciplines has not directly influenced family scholarship?
     a.   Political science
     b.   Psychology
     c.   Anthropology
     d.   Geology

4.   Which method would be most appropriate to study the effects of the amount of pollen in the air on an individual's mood and well-being?
     a.   Survey research
     b.   Controlled experiment
     c.   Unobtrusive research
     d.   Program evaluation

5. Dr. Simon wants to learn more about sexual behavior among teenage boys. Which methodology would she probably use most successfully to gather this type of information?
   a. Controlled experiment
   b. Unobtrusive research
   c. Field research
   d. Survey research

6. Dr. Hidings has become a participant observer among a religious cult group in northern California. He is most likely to report his findings as a(n)
   a. Statistical report
   b. Novel
   c. Ethnography
   d. Academic essay

7. Researchers who wish to study the amount of violence on children's television shows would probably use which method?
   a. Controlled experiment
   b. Content analysis
   c. Participant observation
   d. Program evaluation

8. Which of the following methods would be most appropriate to help researchers understand whether or not abstinence-based sexual education programs are effective?
   a. Unobtrusive research
   b. Survey research
   c. Program evaluation
   d. Field research

9. Which of the following is not an example of a *rite of passage* in today's society?
   a. Funeral
   b. Wedding
   c. Graduation
   d. First sexual experience

10. Which of the following is not one of Murdock's four functions of the family?
    a. Educational
    b. Reproductive
    c. Sexual
    d. Self concept enhancement

11. Which of the following is not one of the major criticisms of functionalism?
    a. Favors the status quo
    b. Organism analogy may not accurately represent society
    c. Focuses on negative aspects of families
    d. May confuse cause and effect

12. George W. Bush's proposed tax cut policies, which eliminate inheritance taxes, would be most criticized using which theory?
    a. Functionalism
    b. Conflict theory
    c. Social exchange theory
    d. Feminist theory

13. Which of the following is not a major concern for feminist scholars?
    a. Gender
    b. Social change
    c. Concept of teleology
    d. Concept of oppression

14. Modes of production are associated with which theory?
    a. Conflict theory
    b. Social exchange theory
    c. Functionalism
    d. Ecological evolutionary theory

15. Jamie is a sixteen-year-old who has recently had her tongue pierced. When asked why she did this, she says it is because "everybody else" has done it. Which theory would best explain Jamie's behavior?
    a. Functionalism
    b. Social exchange
    c. Symbolic interactionism
    d. Family systems

16. The tradition some societies have of have a dowry or "bride price" can best be explained using
    a. Social exchange theory
    b. Symbolic interactionism
    c. Family development theory
    d. Family systems theory

17. The idea that marital satisfaction might be lowest when couples are raising adolescents can best be explained by
   a. Social exchange theory
   b. Symbolic interactionism
   c. Family developmental theory
   d. Family systems theory

18. Approaching the family using the idea that "the whole is more than the sum of its parts" best characterizes
   a. Family systems theory
   b. Symbolic interactionism
   c. Social exchange theory
   d. Functionalism

19. Which of the following is not one of the levels for the scripting model?
   a. Societal
   b. Personal
   c. Institutional
   d. Mutual

20. Billy grew up in a household where members fixed their own meals and ate in front of the TV set. Sammy grew up in a household where one of his parents fixed the meal and everyone ate together at the dining room table. Billy and Sammy consequently will have different _____ scripts around eating.
   a. Societal
   b. Mutual
   c. Personal
   d. Interactive

True/False

1. The scientific method is used to reveal subjective truths.
2. A hypothesis must be testable.
3. The positivist approach to science says science should be value neutral or value free.
4. Anecdotes can often provide sufficient evidence for scientific study.
5. Post-positivist scientists say researchers should be value aware rather than value free.
6. Qualitative data is likely to be summarized using numbers.
7. Random samples are important when evaluating program research.
8. A cross-sectional study records data from people over time.
9. Field research usually produces qualitative data.
10. Content analysis is one type of a controlled experiment.
11. The organismic analogy is used by symbolic interactionists.
12. The concept of dysfunctional family has been developed by the functional perspective.

13. Conflict theorists claim that society tends to favor the "have-nots."
14. Feminists believe that traditional models of objective science are the most appropriate tools for investigation.
15. The development and use of computer technology is of most interest to environmental evolutionary theories.
16. Symbolic interactionism has often been critiqued because it does not focus on or account for larger institutional forces such as police, jails, or mental institutions.
17. The concept of a family as a homeostatic mechanism is part of Simon and Gagnon's scripting model.
18. Societal scripts can be understood using both functionalism and conflict paradigms.
19. Mutual scripts can be understood using symbolic interactionism.
20. Theories provide researchers with concrete ways of organizing information and guiding research.

Matching

The terms introduced in this chapter are listed here in alphabetical order. Match the terms with the appropriate definition.

____	1	Analysis of existing statistics	A	A developmental perspective that focuses on individuals' lives, in their entirety, in historical and social context.
____	2	Androcentric	B	A functionally related group of interacting parts that form a complex whole.
____	3	Anecdotal method	C	A specified set of study units, such as all students attending a certain college.
____	4	Bias	D	A way of finding things out by asking a sample of persons a set of questions.
____	5	Content analysis	E	Expectations learned by socialization and shaped by an individual's unique experiences.
____	6	Controlled experiment	F	Research conducted to determine the effectiveness of some kind of social intervention.
____	7	Cross-sectional studies	G	Studies based on observations representing a single point in time.
____	8	Cultural survival	H	Study of the interaction between persons that takes place through symbols, such as signs, gestures, and language.
____	9	Culture traits	I	The study of recorded human communications, such as books, Web sites, paintings, and laws.
____	10	Developmental paradigm	J	The study of small-scale social processes like face-to-face interaction.

_____	11	Dramaturgy	K	A concept that has more than one attribute.
_____	12	Dysfunction	L	A copy or reproduction; repetition of an experiment or procedure using the same process.
_____	13	Economic determinism	M	**A** culture trait that has survived after its original function has disappeared.
_____	14	Ethnography	N	A form of data gathering in which variables are controlled and manipulated by the researcher.
_____	15	Eufunction	O	A paradigm that focuses on the way various parts of society have consequences that maintain the stability of the whole.
_____	16	Family career	P	A perception or process that results in systematic misrepresentation of reality.
_____	17	Field research	Q	A positive impact on society of a trait or institution.
_____	18	Foraging	R	A study involving the collection of data at different points in time.
_____	19	Function	S	A systematic explanation for the observations about related phenomena.
_____	20	Functionalism	T	A testable educated guess, usually about the relationship among two or more variables.
_____	21	Gynocentric	U	A type of field research on a specific culture or subculture.
_____	22	Homeostasis	V	A type of longitudinal study in which the same people or other cases are observed at different points in time.
_____	23	Humanistic studies	W	A way of understanding ourselves through locating our positions in society, and the social forces that affect us.
_____	24	Hypothesis	X	Collecting plants and animals for subsistence.
_____	25	Impression management	Y	Combining social research and theory with the active attempt to improve society.
_____	26	Life course	Z	Consequence of an action or trait.
_____	27	Longitudinal study	AA	Doctrine emphasizing use of the senses, measurement, and science as a basis for knowledge.
_____	28	Macrosociology	AB	Expectations developed from interaction between specific actors.
_____	29	Microsociology	AC	Explanations of social behavior based on calculation of resources, costs, and benefits of alternative actions.
_____	30	Modes of production	AD	Explanations of social behavior emphasizing stages of life cycles.
_____	31	Mutual script	AE	Finding ways of improving the human condition.
_____	32	Objectivity	AF	Gathering data by direct observation in the natural setting.

____	33	Organismic analogy	AG	Gathering data without influencing the thing being studied.
____	34	Panel study	AH	Interpersonal interaction among more than one individual.
____	35	Personal script	AI	Nonnumeric examination and interpretation of observations.
____	36	Population	AJ	Numerical representation and manipulation of observations.
____	37	Positivism	AK	Process in which a person manipulates others' perceptions of himself or herself to achieve a desired outcome.
____	38	Praxis	AL	Sample in which all units in the population have an equal chance of being selected.
____	39	Program evaluation	AM	Society-wide, macrosocial expectations.
____	40	Qualitative analysis	AN	The assumption that truth resides in the object or phenomenon being studied.
____	41	Quantitative analysis	AO	The assumption that truth resides in the subject or person doing the observing.
____	42	Random sample	AP	The attempt to prove a point by telling a story.
____	43	Replication	AQ	The body of knowledge available to a society that is of use in fashioning implements, practicing arts and skills, and extracting or collecting materials.
____	44	Scene	AR	The division and specialization of social and cultural units such as groups, organizations, and institutions.
____	45	Social differentiation	AS	The entirety of events and stages traversed by a family.
____	46	Social exchange paradigm	AT	The method by which the majority of a society's members produce or develop the goods needed by the society.
____	47	Societal script	AU	The process of social and cultural change in response to the environment, made possible by the accumulation of technical knowledge.
____	48	Sociocultural evolution	AV	The simplest functional units into which a culture is divided for purposes of analysis.
____	49	Sociological imagination	AW	The study of final causes; the belief that events are determined by some ultimate design or purpose.
____	50	Subjectivity	AX	The study of interaction as impression management by an actor for an audience.
____	51	Survey research	AY	The study of the large-scale structures and processes of society.
____	52	Symbolic interactionism	AZ	The tendency of an organism to maintain internal equilibrium by making adjustments to changing

conditions.

_____	53	System	BA	The theory that the economic base of society determines the general character of social structure and culture.
_____	54	Technology	BB	The view that society is like an individual life form, with parts that work together to carry on the various processes of life.
_____	55	Teleology	BC	Those observed consequences that lessen the adaptation or adjustment of the system.
_____	56	Theory	BD	Unaffected by preconceived ideas about what is good, right, and proper.
_____	57	Unobtrusive research	BE	Use of previously completed analysis as the raw data in an original study.
_____	58	Value-free	BF	With men at the center of interest.
_____	59	Variable	BG	With women at the center of interest.

Short Essay

1. Compare and contrast quantitative and qualitative research approaches.
2. Using Lillian Rubin's research as an example, describe at least two advantages and two disadvantages of using ethnography as a research method.
3. After defining functionalism, discuss the major critiques of this theory.
4. Select one of the macro theories discussed in the chapter and outline the nature of the society, the view of social change, the key elements of society, the basic analytic question, and the view of the traditional family.

Critical Thinking

1. After reading some of the information about the Tuskegee Experiment at "Internet Resources on the Tuskegee Study" (http://www.gpc.edu/~shale/humanities/composition/assignments/ experiment/tuskegee.html) or watching the movie *Miss Evers' Boys*, discuss at least two ethical issues involving research with human subjects. What specific ethical violations were there in the study? Could such an "experiment" be performed today?
2. Select a current article from news media on a topic relevant to the scientific study of families. Analyze this article using one of the theories described in this chapter. Do the authors of the article indicate their research methods or theory preferences? How would knowing this information help you to become a better consumer and critic of information?
3. You are interested in conducting survey research with college students regarding their "cheating on tests" behaviors. Design five closed-ended questions and five open-ended

questions that you might use on your survey. What kind of information will each type of question yield? Discuss how you might analyze the results of your survey.

Additional Small Group Discussions

Here are some examples of research questions. Some could best be addressed by only one technique, but others could be approached in a number of different ways. What is the best method for addressing each research question? (Don't try to answer the question—just decide how a researcher would best approach it.)

How much physical abuse is occurring among dating couples on campus? Nationally?
Why do some people join fraternities and sororities while others do not? Are these functional families?
Do students whose parents are divorced have the same kind of college experience as students whose parents never divorced?
Do "abstinence only" sex education programs reduce unwanted pregnancy?
How do married couples usually resolve disagreements about spending money?
What form of mate selection was used by traditional Apaches? How does that compare to today's Apaches?
What impression of men is given by conversations and activities at all-women bridal showers? What impression of women is given by conversation and activities at bachelor parties?
Who is generally happier—married couples, cohabiting couples, or unattached individuals living alone?
Are family types distributed differentially by race and ethnicity?

Answer Keys

Multiple Choice

1.	d	6.	c	11.	c	16.	a
2.	c	7.	b	12.	b	17.	c
3.	d	8.	c	13.	c	18.	a
4.	b	9.	d	14.	d	19.	c
5.	d	10.	d	15.	c	20.	c

True/False

1.	f	6.	f	11.	f	16.	t
2.	t	7.	f	12.	t	17.	f
3.	t	8.	f	13.	f	18.	t
4.	f	9.	t	14.	f	19.	t
5.	t	10.	f	15.	t	20.	f

Matching

1.	BE	13.	BA	25.	AK	37.	AA	49.	W
2.	BF	14.	U	26.	Z	38.	Y	50.	AO
3.	AP	15.	Q	27.	R	39.	F	51.	D
4.	P	16.	AS	28.	AY	40.	AI	52.	H
5.	I	17.	AF	29.	J	41.	AJ	53.	B
6.	N	18.	X	30.	AT	42.	AL	54.	AQ
7.	G	19.	Z	31.	AB	43.	L	55.	AW
8.	M	20.	O	32.	AN	44.	AH	56.	S
9.	AV	21.	BG	33.	BE	45.	AR	57.	AG
10.	AD	22.	AZ	34.	V	46.	AC	58.	BD
11.	AX	23.	AE	35.	E	47.	AM	59.	K
12.	BC	24.	T	36.	C	48.	AU		

Short Essay

1. Compare and contrast quantitative and qualitative research approaches.
    a. Quantitative uses numbers, data, and empirical observation, so can be more easily summarized.
    b. Qualitative usually relies on participant observation, ethnographies, and open-ended interviews.
    c. Quantitative tends to speak more to macro questions while qualitative speaks more to micro questions.
    d. Quantitative searches for objective truths while qualitative reports subjective truths.

2. Using Lillian Rubin's research as an example, describe at least two advantages and two disadvantages of using ethnography as a research method research.
    a. Advantages—captures more detail and the "human" side of research and might be more "readable" than some scientific reports.
    b. Disadvantages—not generalizable and may be considered "anecdotal" and subjective.

3. After defining functionalism, discuss the major critiques of this theory.
    a. Favors status quo.
    b. Organismic analogy may not fit society.
    c. Focuses primarily on good things about families and societies, thus overlooks problems.
    d. Dysfunction implies value-laden judgments.
    e. False teleologies or confusion around cause and effect.

4. Select one of the macro theories discussed in the chapter and outline the nature of the society, the view of social change, the key elements of society, the basic analytic question, and the view of the traditional family.
    a. See table 2.2.

Chapter 3 Families in Preindustrial Context

Learning Objectives

After reading this chapter, you should be able to
1. List salient characteristics of hunter-gatherer societies.
2. Explain gender roles and patterns in hunter-gatherer societies.
3. Discuss social stratification and institution formation in preindustrial societies.
4. Describe family formation processes in preindustrial societies.
5. Locate the origin of the European family historically, including religious influences.
6. Discuss the transitions from Europe to North America in terms of family function and with respect to ethnicity.
7. Explain how kinship patterns influenced mate selection.
8. Compare colonial family functions between New England Puritan families, African American families, and/or Southern White families.

Chapter Outline

Thinking Ahead: If you lived in a hunting-gathering society 15,000 years ago, what do you think your family would be like? How about the colonial North American family? What would your marital role structure be? How would the mate-selection process work? Would you prefer that life, or the one you have today? Why?

1) Overview of Preindustrial Societies
    a) Life as a hunter-gatherer
    b) Transition to agrarian societies

2) Preindustrial Institutions
    a) Political institutions
    b) Social stratification system
    c) Religion
    d) Education and socialization
    e) Sexuality
        i) Reproduction
        ii) Nonreproductive sexual functions

3) Kinship Systems and Families
    a) Oglala example
    b) Characteristics of agrarian families

4) Family formation
    a) Number of partners
    b) Mate selection

5) The European Family
   a)   The Roman family
   b)   Christian influence
        i)   Marriage as sacrament
        ii)   Monogamous marriage only
        iii) No divorce
        iv)   Sex limiting
        v)   Oppose contraception, abortion and infanticide
   c)   Changes in inheritance
   d)   Households
   e)   Gender
   f)   Children

6) The North American Family
   a)   Puritan New England families
   b)   African American slave families
   c)   Southern White families

Rethinking in Context: Now that you have read the chapter, have you changed your mind about living in a hunting-gathering society? In colonial America? Specifically, what traits would you like? What traits would you dislike? On what values are you basing your choices?

Multiple Choice Questions

1.   Much of the information we have about hunting-gathering and early horticultural societies comes from
     a.   Historical sociologists
     b.   Ethnographies written by anthropologists
     c.   Sociobiologists
     d.   News reports

2.   Which of the following are typical characteristics of hunting-gathering societies?
     a.   Small group size
     b.   Simple technology
     c.   Frequent migration
     d.   All of the above

3.   According to Murdock's study, which of the following is most true?
     a.   Men never foraged for food
     b.   Women made most of the tools
     c.   Men regularly engaged in child care
     d.   Women usually tended the shelter and did most of the cooking

4.. Which of the following developments help people make the transitions from hunting-gathering societies to horticultural-based communities?
    a. Developing a monogamous family form
    b. Advanced knowledge about hunting techniques
    c. Introducing metals into tool production
    d. Developing a written language

5. Which factor was the most influential in leading to specialized occupations?
    a. Finding constant water sources
    b. Eating more nutritious food
    c. Extended life expectancies
    d. Food surplus

6. Some theorists propose that the social importance of the family began to decrease as _____ began to increase.
    a. Food supplies
    b. Social institutions
    c. Gender role specialization
    d. Permanent shelters

7. Warfare was most common in which type of society?
    a. Hunting and gathering
    b. Simple horticultural
    c. Advanced horticultural
    d. Warfare was equally common in all types of society.

8. Social stratification means
    a. Everyone is treated equally in the society
    b. Men have power over women
    c. Women have power over men
    d. People are ranked hierarchically, based on wealth, power, or prestige

9. Most cultures have sought answers to question concerning life, death, and the origins of humans. These ideas are often represented in
    a. Carvings on tools
    b. Creation myths and stories
    c. Ancestral worship practices

10. The idea of a supreme being or creator was most common in which type of society?
    a. Agrarian societies
    b. Hunting-gathering societies
    c. Simple horticultural societies
    d. Advanced horticultural societies

11.   Formal education was accelerated by the development of
    a.   A more efficient hunting technique
    b.   Writing
    c.   Religious institutions
    d.   Apprenticeships

12.   Birth control practices were common in
    a.   Hunting-gathering societies
    b.   Simple horticultural societies
    c.   Agrarian societies
    d.   All of the above

13.   The example of berdache found in many Native American communities illustrates
    a.   The complexity and fluidity of gender role assignment
    b.   The importance of social stratification
    c.   Ethnocentrism on the part of ethnographers
    d.   The growth of the educational institution

14.   Matrilineality and patrilocality were more common in
    a.   Hunter-gatherer societies
    b.   Simple agrarian societies
    c.   Horticultural societies
    d.   Industrial societies

15.   Patrilineality and patrilocality were more common in
    a.   Hunter-gatherer societies
    b.   Simple agrarian societies
    c.   Horticultural societies
    d.   None of the above

16.   According to Murdock's summary study, which family formation was most common?
    a.   Group marriage
    b.   Polygyny
    c.   Polyandry
    d.   Multilateral

17.   Familia was a term used by Roman families to represent
    a.   Biological kinship relationships
    b.   Male heads of household
    c.   All members of a household, including slaves and servants
    d.   All of the above

18. Which of the following is not one of the major impacts Christianity had on family development?
   a. Monogamy became the norm
   b. Abortion became more acceptable
   c. Marriage became a sacrament
   d. Sexual behavior outside of marriage was restricted

19. "Coverture" is a term that means
   a. You should not covet your neighbor's wife
   b. A wife is not allowed to own property of her own
   c. Raising children is solely the women's responsibility
   d. Public displays of affection are illegal

20. Puritan New England families thought that children
   a. Were innocent and carefree
   b. Were inherently sinful and needed to be "tamed"
   c. Were naturally respectful and obedient
   d. None of the above

21. African American slave couples often celebrated marriages, even though they were not legal, by
   a. Church weddings
   b. Jumping over a broomstick together
   c. Escaping from the plantation
   d. Worshiping their ancestors

22. Challenges that Southern White families faced included
   a. More disease than in New England
   b. Malnutrition
   c. Higher mortality rates
   d. All of the above.

True/False

1. Nomadic groups often had many specialized tools.
2. Agrarian communities remained small so as not to deplete food resources.
3. Strict discipline of boys became more evident in societies with a military emphasis.
4. The most extreme differences in family wealth and poverty probably can be found in advanced agrarian societies just before industrialization.
5. Totemism was most common in horticultural societies.
6. "Be fruitful and multiply" was a principle found in polytheistic communities.
7. Infanticide was common in many preindustrial societies.

8. The Oglala example of kinship illustrates how incest taboos differ depending on family relationships and customs.
9. Polyandry is quite common in pre-industrial communities.
10. Preference for marriage to a "cross cousin" is an example of a prescriptive norm.

Matching

The terms introduced in this chapter are listed here in alphabetical order. Match the terms with the appropriate definition.

_____	1	Animism	A	A marriage with one husband and more than one wife.
_____	2	Annulment	B	A proclamation that a marriage was agreed to and would occur.
_____	3	Banns	C	Official declaration that a supposed marriage was never valid.
_____	4	Berdache	D	A belief that there is only one appropriate religion for all people everywhere.
_____	5	Bundling	E	A courting custom by which a couple would spend an evening together in bed, but fully clothed, separated by a "bundling board" or other material.
_____	6	Chivalry	F	A group of kin who believe themselves related to a common, sometimes mythological, ancestor.
_____	7	Clan	G	A marriage involving more than one husband and more than one wife.
_____	8	Concordia	H	A marriage involving one wife and more than one husband
_____	9	Concubine	I	A payment at marriage from the groom's *familias* to the bride.
_____	10	Courtship	J	A person who acts as a medium between the visible world and the invisible world of the spirits.
_____	11	Coverture	K	A person, usually male, who was anatomically normal but assumed the dress, occupations, and behavior of the other sex to effect a change in gender status.
_____	12	Cross cousins	L	A sacred tale expressing the unobservable realities of religious belief in terms of observable phenomena.
_____	13	Demographics	M	A state of harmony and lack of disagreement between Roman husband and wife.
_____	14	Demography	N	A woman who cohabits with a man; a live-in mistress.
_____	15	Divorce	O	An official end of a marriage.
_____	16	Donatio	P	Any marriage with more than two partners.
_____	17	Familia	Q	Belief in only one god.
_____	18	Gens	R	Characteristics of human populations.

____	19	Group marriage	S	Expectations about what *should* be done.
____	20	Infanticide	T	Expectations about what *should not* be done.
____	21	Kinship system	U	Latin word for the group of slaves and servants in the household; came to refer to the household as a whole.
____	22	Life chances	V	Marriage with one husband and one wife.
____	23	Monogamy	W	Medieval norms of knighthood, including bravery, courtesy, honor, and gallantry toward women.
____	24	Monotheism	X	Member of the Roman aristocracy; the ruling class from which Senators came.
____	25	Myth	Y	Moving as a group from place to place in search of food, water, or grazing land.
____	26	Nomadic	Z	One's mother's brother's or father's sister's children.
____	27	Parallel cousins	AA	One's mother's sister's or father's brother's children.
____	28	Paterfamilias	AB	Remaining in one place; not migratory.
____	29	Patrician	AC	Roman clan; group of persons of both *gen*ders who believe themselves to share a common *gen*esis for many *gen*erations, and who treat each other *gen*tly.
____	30	Polyandry	AD	Socially scripted process by which potentially sexual pairs interact to form relationships that can result in marriage.
____	31	Polygamy	AE	Symbolic representation that links individuals or groups with human ancestors, plants, animals, or other natural phenomena.
____	32	Polygyny	AF	The belief in many gods.
____	33	Polytheism	AG	The belief that spirits reside in all aspects of nature.
____	34	Prescriptive norms	AH	The doctrine that a man and woman become one flesh at marriages, with the consequence that a wife's property rights are controlled by her husband.
____	35	Primogeniture	AI	The hierarchical ranking of individuals on the basis of wealth, power, or prestige.
____	36	Proscriptive norms	AJ	The killing of infants, usually as a population control mechanism.
____	37	Sedentary	AK	The male head of household.
____	38	Shaman	AL	The probability a person has of sharing in the economic and cultural goods of a society.
____	39	Social stratification	AM	The right of the eldest child, especially the eldest son, to inherit all property of the parents.
____	40	Totem	AN	The study of the characteristics of populations, including birthrates, death rates, growth, and vital statistics.

_____   41   Universal faith   AO   The way in which a society defines the relationships of those who are inter-related by blood, marriage, or adoption.

Short Essay

1. Discuss division of labor by gender in typical hunting-gathering societies.
2. Select at least one example provided in the text of nonreproductive sexual behavior and describe how this may or may not have impacted family development.
3. Describe the five major effects Christianity had on European and American family systems.
4. Discuss how primogeniture laws influenced family development in twelfth-century Europe.

Critical Thinking

1. Using one of the ethnographic examples described at (http://www.umanitoba.ca/facuties/arts/anthropology/tutor/kinmenu.html), discuss parallel cousin marriages and whether or not this particular society views these as desirable marriages and why.

2. Construct a genogram of your own family system for at least three generations (You can get assistance at http://faculty-web.at.northwestern.edu/commstud/galvin/genograms/Basic%20Genogram%20Components.htm. After creating a chart or graph of your family, select one of the following themes to discuss in a two or three page essay:
    a. Attitudes toward money
    b. Religious affiliations
    c. Patterns of work or occupations
    d. Educational goals or experience
    e. Military experiences
    f. Attitudes toward sex
    g. Attitudes toward health

3. Which of the macro-sociological theories discussed in Chapter 2 of this text best explain the gendered division of labor found in the various types of preindustrial societies? Support your position.

Additional Small Group Discussions

Here is a science fiction scenario called the "last class on earth" exercise. For reasons you can't determine, you discover after class one day that the students in your class seem to be the only remaining people alive. No bodies are found, but there are no live people anywhere. You can't contact anyone on your cell phones, and no live broadcasts can be located on radio or television, etc. Your small group has been named by the others in the class to establish norms designed to ensure that the human race will continue. Keep in mind that the technology you are used to will soon be lost—electricity will shut down, gas and water supplies will disappear for lack of maintenance, etc.

Canned food is widely available in grocery stores and elsewhere, but even that will eventually go bad. So what mode of production will you need to develop? More importantly, how will the family system be arranged? Who will reproduce, and with whom, and under what kind of marital rules? What normative structure or laws will be developed, and how will that be enforced? What will happen with the other social institutions? Will production be privately owned, or will everything be shared?

Answer Keys

Multiple Choice

1.	b	7.	c	13.	a	19.	b
2.	d	8.	d	14.	c	20.	b
3.	d	9.	b	15.	b	21.	b
4.	c	10.	a	16.	b	22.	d
5.	d	11.	b	17.	c		
6.	b	12.	d	18.	b		

True/False

1.	f		6.	f
2.	f		7.	t
3.	t		8.	t
4.	t		9.	f
5.	t		10.	t

Matching

1.	AG	11.	AH	21.	AO	31.	P
2.	C	12.	Z	22.	AL	32.	A
3.	B	13.	R	23.	V	33.	AF
4.	K	14.	AN	24.	Q	34.	S
5.	E	15.	O	25.	L	35.	AM
6.	W	16.	I	26.	Y	36.	T
7.	F	17.	U	27.	AA	37.	AB
8.	M	18.	AC	28.	AK	38.	J
9.	N	19.	G	29.	X	39.	AI
10.	AD	20.	AJ	30.	H	40.	AE
						41.	D

Short Essay

1. Discuss division of labor by gender in typical hunting-gathering societies.
   a. Men hunted and fished
   b. Women gathered fruits, nuts, plants, and small animals
   c. Women were primary child tenders
   d. Women tended the shelter and did most of the cooking
   e. If warfare, men were warriors

2. Select at least one example provided in the text of nonreproductive sexual behavior and describe how this may or may not have impacted family development
   a. North American Plains Tribes—ritual intercourse with wife of younger man; illustrates passing of power to younger generation
   b. Sambian Melanesian society—symbolic importance of body fluids; oral sex provided method of transmission of power to younger generations
   c. Native American berdache—challenges traditional gender roles; focuses both on relational aspects and sexual behaviors

3. Describe the five major effects Christianity had on European and American family systems.
   a. Marriage as sacrament
   b. Monogamous marriage only
   c. No divorce
   d. Sex-limiting
   e. Opposed contraception, abortion, infanticide

4. Discuss how primogeniture laws influenced family development in twelfth-century Europe.
   a. Small group of nobility owned most of land
   b. Having legitimate heirs became very important
   c. Younger siblings had no means of support
   d. Parents made alliance with wealthy families by bartering daughters for marriage

Chapter 4 Industrialization and Families

Learning Objectives

After reading this chapter, you should be able to
1. Discuss how changes in economic institutions affected families during industrialization, particularly with respect to women in the labor force.
2. Describe how the Protestant Reformation and secularization impacted family functioning.
3. Explain the changing role of government and education during industrialization.
4. Outline Goode's four major points with respect to families and industrialization.
5. Describe at least one group of people who did not follow typical patterns with respect to industrialization (Oneida community or Mormons).
6. Discuss how industrialization was different in noncapitalist societies.
7. Describe China's one-child law and its effects on families.

Chapter Outline

Thinking Ahead: Imagine that you are responsible for explaining your life and society to a hunter-gatherer and an agrarian who have both been transported into their future, which is your present. How would you explain what you do every day? How would you explain your family and other relationships? Are there some things that might be very difficult for your visitors to understand?

1) Industrial Institutions
    a) The economic institution
        i) Phase 1 (1760–1850)
        ii) Phase 2 (1850–1900)
        iii) Phase 3 (1900–1940)
        iv) Phase 4 (1940–1970)
        v) The industrial workforce
    b) The religious institution
        i) The Protestant Reformation
        ii) Secularization
    c) Political institutions
    d) The educational institution
    e) Demographic changes
        i) Population growth
        ii) Migration
        iii) Life expectancy

2) Industrialization and Families
    a) Goode's Family Analysis
        i) Geographic mobility

      ii)   Social mobility
      iii) "Achieved" occupational status
      iv) Specialization and function differentiation
  b) The conjugal family form
      i)   More nuclear and less extended
      ii)   Kinship more bilateral
      iii) Mate selection based on choice
      iv) Economic exchanges at marriage disappear
      v)   Families become more egalitarian
  c) Treatment of children

3) The Industrialization Backlash in North America
  a) The Oneida Community
  b) Mormons
      i)   Polygyny
      ii) Celestial marriage
      iii) Gender roles

4) Noncapitalist Industrialization and Families: The Soviet Union

5) Noncapitalist Industrialization and Families: China
  a) Traditional China
      i)   The Tsu
      ii) Religion
  b) The traditional family
  c) The family in the People's Republic of China
      i)   Institutional context
      ii) Family changes
      iii) The one-child policy

Rethinking in Context: How is a "successful" life defined in an industrial society? A hunting-gathering society? An agrarian society? What characteristics are necessary to achieve that success in each society? How does the family into which one is born affect one's chances of having the characteristics that lead to success in each society?

Multiple Choice Questions

1.   The steam engine is the most significant development of which stage of industrialization?
      a.   Phase 1
      b.   Phase 2
      c.   Phase 3
      d.   Phase 4

2. Corporations with professional managers began during which stage of industrialization
    a. Phase 1
    b. Phase 2
    c. Phase 3
    d. Phase 4

3. Electricity and advanced technology were characteristics of which stage of industrialization?
    a. Phase 1
    b. Phase 2
    c. Phase 3
    d. Phase 4

4. Development of labor-saving machines was characteristic of which stage of industrialization?
    a. Phase 1
    b. Phase 2
    c. Phase 3
    d. Phase 4

5. Which of the following statements is most true?
    a. Women and children were not allowed to work in early factories
    b. Few women were in the labor force until after WWII
    c. Development of the telephone and typewriter opened new fields of employment for women
    d. The family wage movement demanded jobs for all family members

6. Which of the following is not one of Weber's beliefs regarding the Protestant Reformation?
    a. Protestants believed that work is punishment for sin
    b. Protestants believed in a personal relationship with God
    c. Protestants believed they could improve their life while on earth
    d. Protestants emphasized denial of pleasure

7. Which of the following statements is most true?
    a. Early agrarian societies are the most democratic
    b. There is a relationship between the development of democracy and industrialization
    c. Democracy was started by slaves and poor people who wanted a better life
    d. The development of democracy and expanded public education are unrelated

8. Compulsory education for primary-age students happened
   a. By the Civil War
   b. Before 1800
   c. By World War I
   d. During the Korean War

9. Population during industrialization
   a. Increased slightly
   b. Increased significantly
   c. Decreased slightly
   d. Decreased significantly

10. One of the strongest factors for increasing life expectancy was
    a. Urbanization
    b. Migration
    c. Germ theory of disease
    d. Better nutrition

11. Which of the following is not one of Goode's major points about industrialization and families?
    a. Industrial economies require geographic mobility
    b. Industrialization requires social mobility
    c. Industrialization requires arranged marriage
    d. Industrialization increases specialization

12. Which of the following is not a characteristic of nuclear families due to industrialization?
    a. They became smaller
    b. There were more children
    c. They became more socially isolated
    d. The family was seen as a retreat from work

13. Which of the following is most true regarding mate selection during industrialization?
    a. Young adults were freer to pick their own mates
    b. Parents had more control and arranged marriages
    c. "Romantic love" was not a criteria for mate selection
    d. Young adults married at younger ages

14. The "cult of domesticity" refers to a
    a. Religious group
    b. Glorified role of homemaker and mother
    c. Group of domestic workers
    d. Method of raising tame animals

15.   Which of the following groups did not try to preserve pre-industrial family scripts?
    a.   Amish
    b.   Hutterites
    c.   Oneida community
    d.   Hasidim

16.   Which of the following is not a characteristic of the Oneida community?
    a.   People lived in individual housing units
    b.   One of the goals of the community was to improve themselves biologically in future generations
    c.   Children were raised communally
    d.   Sexuality was most often expressed in terms of control and restraint

17.   Which of the following is most true concerning the Mormon practice of Polygyny?
    a.   Almost all husbands had multiple wives
    b.   A present wife had to give her permission before additional wives could be married
    c.   Traditional gender roles are unusual in Mormon families
    d.   Polygyny is currently legal in the state of Utah

18.   Which of the following is not a characteristic of the changes communism brought to the Soviet Union?
    a.   Divorces became more readily available
    b.   Abortion was legalized
    c.   Legal obligations between parents and children in terms of inheritance were minimized
    d.   Religion and the church assumed a larger role in the community

19.   Which of the following statements is most true about traditional Chinese families?
    a.   Most were monogamous but sometimes wealthy women had multiple husbands
    b.   Marriages were usually arranged
    c.   Women usually married in their late twenties
    d.   Class was not a relevant issue to marriage alliances

20.   Which of the following is most true about the communist revolution in China?
    a.   There was no emphasis on gender equality
    b.   Individuals were encouraged to choose their own mates
    c.   Divorces were difficult to obtain
    d.   Wealthy families continued to hold most of the power

True/False

1. During industrialization, it became higher status if men could earn enough money so that women and children in the household did not have to work.
2. In the year 2005, over 60% of women are in the paid labor force.
3. Protestants believed in hard work and the denial of pleasure.
4. The number of people who attend church and say they believe in God historically has declined since 1776.
5. Education and industrialization expanded at the same time because many jobs required more skills and literacy.
6. The idea of keeping family property or estates for centuries was important to the early American experience of industrialization.
7. Women were usually awarded custody of young children after phase two of industrialization.
8. Most of the positions of power within the Mormon Church were held equally by men and women.
9. A major goal of communism was to replace private property with state-owned or communal property.
10. Chinese families prefer to have girl children.

Matching

The terms introduced in this chapter are listed here in alphabetical order. Match the terms with the appropriate definition.

____	1	Achieved status	A	A demographic calculation of the number of males per 100 females in a given population.
____	2	Ascribed status	B	A social position that is assigned to the individual at birth or other life stage, based on criteria over which the individual has no control.
____	3	Calling	C	A social position that results from a person's own life events.
____	4	Capitalism	D	A type of extended family composed of the parents plus only one child, who might marry and have children.
____	5	Democracy	E	An economic system in which production and distribution are controlled by private individuals or groups and guided by the profit motive.
____	6	Eugenics	F	An increase in the percentage of a population living in cities.
____	7	Filial piety	G	Central Confucian ideal involving devotion and reverence of a son to his father; extended to other dominant-subordinate relationships.

____	8	Modified-extended family	H	Christians who are the theological descendants of Martin Luther, John Calvin, or Ulrich Zwingli. For practical purposes, a member of any Christian denomination that is not Catholic.
____	9	Protestants	I	Government by the people.
____	10	Secularization	J	In Protestant theology, an occupation to which one could be "called" by God.
____	11	Sex ratio	K	Nuclear family that retains considerable autonomy but maintains emotional and economic ties to other related groups.
____	12	Stem family	L	Taoist unity of opposites: female-male; dark-light; passive-active; moon-sun.
____	13	Tender years rule	M	The Chinese version of the *gens* or clan.
____	14	Tsu	N	The norm that, in divorce, a mother should automatically get custody of minor children unless proven unfit.
____	15	Urbanization	O	The process by which religious control over social institutions and individual behavior declines.
____	16	Yin-yang principle	P	The study of hereditary improvement of the human species by controlled selective breeding.

Short Essay

1. List at least two ways secularization changed the family during industrialization.
2. Discuss the research controversies regarding the treatment of children during industrialization
3. Discuss how industrialization changed the role of women in the family.

Critical Thinking

1. Using the criteria posted at "Cults 101: Checklist of Cult Characteristics" (http://www.csj.org/infoserv_cult101/checklis.htm) or a similar Web site of your choice, discuss whether or not you think the Oneida community or the Mormons meet the definition of a cult. How would "cult" membership impact family construction and/or membership? Additional information on these groups can be found on sites such as "The Oneida Community" (http://nyhistory.com/central/oneida/htm) or "All About Mormons" (http://www.mormons.org).

2. If the United States were to implement a "one-child" policy similar to that of China, how would you envision this changing family configuration, values, and/or public policies?

3. Referring to the section about research methods in Chapter 2, how do you think most of the information in Chapter 4 was originally gathered? Why? Include mention of specific pieces of information linked to specific methods.

Additional Small Group Discussions

Continue the "Last Class on Earth" exercise you started in Chapter 3. What elements of industrial production might you be able to save? Will you continue to teach the children, who will have no knowledge of the technology you took for granted, to read and write? If so, will any of the pre-disaster knowledge be useful to them? How are incestuous relationships likely to be defined and avoided? How will the political institution be likely to develop? Will gender equality continue to be an important value?

Answer Keys

Multiple Choice

1.	a	6.	a	11.	c	16.	a
2.	b	7.	b	12.	b	17.	b
3.	b	8.	c	13.	a	18.	d
4.	a	9.	b	14.	b	19.	b
5.	c	10.	c	15.	c	20.	b

True/False

1.	t	6.	f
2.	t	7.	t
3.	t	8.	f
4.	f	9.	t
5.	t	10.	f

Matching

1.	C	9.	H
2.	B	10.	O
3.	J	11.	A
4.	E	12.	D
5.	I	13.	N
6.	P	14.	M
7.	G	15.	F
8.	K	16.	L

Short Essay

1. List at least two ways secularization changed the family during industrialization.
    - a. Valid marriages no longer demanded religious ceremonies.
    - b. Daily events lost their religious significance.
    - c. Scientists developed rational explanations for natural phenomena.

2. Discuss the research controversies regarding the treatment of children during industrialization
    - a. The "indifference" position says children were mistreated, abused, and neglected.
    - b. Some researchers said good mothering was an invention of industrialization but was based on class differences.
    - c. Other researchers said the human race would not have survived if children had been so grossly mistreated.
    - d. Changes in child labor laws provide evidence of change during industrialization.

3. Discuss how industrialization changed the role of women in the family.
    - a. Especially during WWII more women entered the paid labor force.
    - b. Families became smaller in size.
    - c. The home became a "haven" from work-related activities.
    - d. More labor-saving devices became available.

Chapter 5 Gender, Work, and Postindustrial Families

Learning Objectives

After reading this chapter, you should be able to
1. Discuss how changes in the economy impacted families in the postindustrial revolution.
2. Explain how religious institutions, particularly with relation to churchgoers versus nonchurchgoers, have affected families.
3. Relate how education is becoming a lifelong necessity.
4. Associate demographic trends with changes in family functioning.
5. Outline the rationale behind the earning gap between men and women from both the discrimination perspective and the human capital perspective.
6. Discuss the danger gap in relation to gender and work.
7. Briefly explain the history of housework, including "emotional work."
8. Explain gender differences in marital role structures and scripts.
9. Describe work-family impacts on children.
10. Compare nonindustrialized patterns using Sub-Saharan Africa as an example.
11. Discuss Sweden as an example of a highly developed country.

Chapter Outline

Thinking Ahead: Considering the long-term trends that have occurred in the family in the past, what would the family be like in the future if the trends continued? Could any recent changes in technology affect those trends?

1) The Postindustrial Revolution
    a)   The economic institution
    b)   The religious institution
    c)   The educational institution
    d)   Demographics

2) Men and Women in the Paid Labor Force
    a)   Labor force participation
    b)   The earnings gap
        i)   The discrimination perspective
        ii)   The human capital perspective
        iii) The danger gap

3) Women and Men in the Family Workforce
    a)   History of housework
    b)   Scripting the marital role structure
        i)   Complementary scripts
        ii)   Part-time or shift work
        iii) Parallel scripts

    c) A second shift?
    d) Negotiating gendered housework
    e) Other family-work scripts
    f) Work-family impacts on children
    g) The future of work and the family

4) Economy and Family in Global Perspective
    a) Selected international comparison
    b) Today's nonindustrialized patterns: Sub-Saharan Africa
    c) Swedish family scripts

Rethinking in Context: Given the current workforce structure, if a mother takes time and energy away from work to devote time to her children, she is likely to suffer long-term lower earnings than would a man or woman who devotes full-time energies to their careers. Is it worth the sacrifice? Why are men less likely to make the same sacrifice? How are the children affected by this? Should changes be made to this situation? If so, what?

Multiple Choice Questions

1. In the postindustrial revolution, which types of jobs have declined in number?
    a. Information occupations
    b. Manufacturing jobs
    c. Clerical work
    d. Service jobs

2. Young adults today are likely to
    a. Be married longer than their parents
    b. Live with their parents longer
    c. Have more children than their parents did
    d. Get less education

3. Churchgoers are more likely to
    a. Be single
    b. Have more children than nonchurchgoers
    c. Be liberal politically
    d. Favor nontraditional gender roles

4. The average age of college students is
    a. Declining
    b. Remaining the same
    c. Increasing

5.   In terms of demographics and marriage rates, most Americans will
      a.   Never get married
      b.   Marry under the age of twenty
      c.   Marry during their late twenties
      d.   Marry in their thirties

6.   The most rapid change in terms of women entering the paid labor force is _____ entering the labor force.
      a.   Single mothers
      b.   Married women
      c.   Women over thirty-five
      d.   Women with preschool-age children

7.   The discrimination perspective on the wage gap supports which of the following concepts?
      a.   Human capital
      b.   Glass ceiling
      c.   Women perform inferior work
      d.   None of the above

8.   The human capital perspective on the wage gap explains the differences in wages based on
      a.   Hours worked
      b.   Years of experience and on the job
      c.   Career choice
      d.   All of the above

9.   In terms of the number of hours spent doing housework, there has been
      a.   An increase in time
      b.   A decrease in time
      c.   Relatively no change since the 1930s

10.   In the case of a divorce, people in which of the following marital scripts are at more financial risk?
      a.   Parallel scripts
      b.   Complementary scripts
      c.   Single income family

11.   A marital partner who relocates with her or his partner, often giving up her or his own career, is called a
     a.   Secondary spouse
     b.   Trailing spouse
     c.   Unsynchronized spouse
     d.   Commuter spouse

12.   Research on marital satisfaction in commuter marriages suggests
     a.   Couples are very satisfied
     b.   Less satisfaction with life in general
     c.   Couples derive most satisfaction from their relationships
     d.   All of the above

13.   Who is more likely to experience role conflict?
     a.   Working women who are mothers
     b.   Working men who are fathers
     c.   Childless working women
     d.   Childless working men

14.   Men who do housework and child care while their partners are the breadwinners
     a.   Are increasing in number
     b.   Are rapidly becoming the first choice among married couples
     c.   Represent between 2% and 3% of households
     d.   None of the above

15.   When observing patterns of housework done by teenagers
     a.   Boys do more than girls
     b.   Girls do more than boys
     c.   Boys and girls do equal amounts

16.   In the Sub-Saharan Africa example
     a.   Families are seen as less important than work
     b.   Marriages between different ethnic groups are common
     c.   Men grow most of the crops
     d.   Men have greatest access to education, power, and authority

17.   In Sweden, there is (are)
     a.   A high rate of cohabitation
     b.   Many unwanted pregnancies
     c.   Very poor health care
     d.   A rapidly increasing birthrate

18. Which of the following is most true about the postindustrial revolution?
    a. It has been characterized by growth in the agricultural industries
    b. It has been characterized by growth in manufacturing jobs
    c. It has been characterized by growth in the information and services industries
    d. It has no relationship to the industries in which people find employment

19. "Baby Boomers" are who?
    a. People who have more than three children
    b. People who have their first child before age eighteen
    c. People born between 1946 and 1964
    d. People who have both young children and older parents to care for

20. Which statement is most true?
    a. While many mothers are in the paid labor force, they are still expected to be primarily responsible for most unpaid family work
    b. Gender discrimination no longer exists
    c. Women now constitute a majority of those in the most dangerous occupations
    d. All the above are true

True/False

1. In terms of economic trends during the postindustrial revolution, the rich are getting richer and the poor are getting poorer.
2. Differences between Catholics and Protestants have been increasing in recent years.
3. A person born in 2050 can expect to live to be 100 years old.
4. Fertility rates have increased during the postindustrial revolution.
5. Labor force participation has not changed much for single mothers from 1980 to 2005.
6. The gender-based wage gap is the same for Blacks and Hispanics as for Whites.
7. Sex discrimination lawsuits are easy to win in civil courts.
8. Several studies have suggested that at entry-level positions in the same jobs, women and men are paid equally.
9. Men and women are likely to participate equally in caring for aging relatives.
10. Child care by fathers is likely to increase for shift workers.

Matching

The terms introduced in this chapter are listed here in alphabetical order. Match the terms with the appropriate definition.

_____	1 Career	A	An age group with care-taking responsibilities both to their aging parents and their own offspring.
_____	2 Commuter marriages	B	A role relationship in which actors assume the same, identical, interchangeable roles.

_____	3	Complementary script	C	A role that holds family and relationships together by communication and organization.
_____	4	Emotion work	D	Husband or wife of an income-producer who relocates for employment purposes.
_____	5	Family leave	E	A leave from employment for family matters, especially the birth of a child.
_____	6	Glass ceiling	F	A long-term professional or occupational path with commitment and opportunities for promotion, advancement, and change.
_____	7	Human capital	G	A prediction that comes true because of the effect of the prediction itself.
_____	8	Kin keeper	H	A role relationship in which actors assume different roles, but those roles mesh with and support one another.
_____	9	Mommy track	I	An alleged invisible barrier to women's advancement in the workforce.
_____	10	Parallel scripts	J	Any work schedule in which more than half of an employee's hours are before 8 am or after 4 pm (Bureau of Labor Statistics).
_____	11	Role conflict	K	Career path that would allow more time for families.
_____	12	Sandwich generation	L	Dual-career marriages in which husband and wife live separately.
_____	13	Self-fulfilling prophecy	M	Efforts to shape and control one's emotions by socially defining them, through conversations or personal reflections on one's feelings.
_____	14	Shift work	N	Incompatibility between two or more roles that an individual is expected to play.
_____	15	Trailing spouse	O	Potential means of production held by an individual that was acquired through formal training, education, or experience.

Short Essay

1. Discuss the changing attitudes women have had about entering the paid labor force.
2. Compare the different explanations of the discrimination perspective versus the human capital perspective on the wage gap.
3. How does "doing gender" impact marital scripts? Be sure to discuss complementary versus parallel scripts.

Critical Thinking

1. Your textbook suggests there is a "danger gap" in relationship to employment risk and behavior. Discuss how you think socialization or "doing gender" may contribute to more men entering more dangerous occupations.

2. Consider how a same sex couple might "do gender." Is the traditional family/work script (complementary or parallel) ignored, maintained, or modified? You may need to do some additional research to support your positions (try www.planetout.com or studies by Lawrence A. Kurdek).
3. Think about the career that you are preparing for. What social forces affected that "choice"? Include a consideration of gender, mode of production, educational, religious, and financial factors in your family of orientation.

Additional Small Group Discussions

What type of work-family script would you like to have when (if) you get married? Why? What are the advantages and disadvantages of that script? Would that change if you have children? If both of you work, who will take care of the child? If one of you does not work, or works less, in order to care for the child, what is the lifetime family financial cost likely to be? What part does gender play in all this, especially the "sex-irreducible" gender roles?

Answer Keys

Multiple Choice

1.	b	6.	d	11.	b	16.	d
2.	b	7.	b	12.	b	17.	a
3.	b	8.	d	13.	a	18.	c
4.	c	9.	c	14.	c	19.	c
5.	c	10.	b	15.	b	20.	a

True/False

1.	t	6.	f
2.	f	7.	f
3.	t	8.	t
4.	f	9.	f
5.	t	10.	t

Matching

1.	F	9.	K
2.	L	10.	B
3.	H	11.	N
4.	M	12.	A
5.	E	13.	G
6.	I	14.	J
7.	O	15.	D
8.	C		

Short Essay

1. Discuss the changing attitudes women have had about entering the paid labor force.
   a. Initially to supplement partner's income
   b. Entered into more professional occupations and had career plan of their own
   c. Need to support self and children due to divorce and single parenthood

2. Compare the different explanations of the discrimination perspective versus the human capital perspective on the wage gap.
   a. Discrimination: main reason for difference is patriarchal society, tradition, laws exist but hard to enforce
   b. Human capital: main reason for wage differences is differences in hours worked, years of experience, years on the job, and choice of different kinds of careers.

3. How does "doing gender" impact marital scripts? Be sure to discuss complementary versus parallel scripts.
   a. Each partner brings notions of gender to relationship
   b. Complementary scripts have partners specializing in certain tasks, often following more traditional gender role scripts—individuals define themselves and their partners to be congruent with scripts
   c. Parallel scripts suggest partners are interchangeable; both must continually behave in ways to conform to that definition of selves

Chapter 6 Social Class and Families

Learning Objectives

After reading this chapter, you should be able to
1. Describe the differences between open and closed mobility systems in addition to explaining the concepts of ascription and meritocracy.
2. Discuss some of the explanations of inequality, including conflict theory, functionalism, cultural factors, and individual reasons.
3. Explain the distribution of wealth in the United States and Weber's theories about it.
4. Relate how occupation, power, and education contribute to social class positions.
5. Discuss the ways poverty can be defined and measured, and how government can respond to poverty.
6. Discuss recent trends in poverty, including the gender gap.
7. Describe some of the characteristics and values of working-class families.
8. Contrast working-class families with middle- and upper-middle-class families.

Chapter Outline

Thinking Ahead: In what ways might your values, norms, and family life have been different had you been born among the very poorest of Americans? How about the very richest? What life advantages and disadvantages came to you from your family of orientation?

1) Why Social Inequality?
   a) Types of stratification systems
   b) Explanations of inequality
      i) Structural explanations: conflict theory
      ii) Structural explanations: functionalism
      iii) Cultural explanations
      iv) Individual explanations

2) Social Class in the United States
   a) Money
   b) Occupation and social class
   c) Power and social class
   d) Formal education and social class

3) Poverty and Families
   a) Who are the poor?
   b) Recent trends in poverty
   c) The poverty gender gap
   d) Welfare and families

4) Working-Class Families

5) The Middle and Upper Classes
   a)   Upper middle class
   b)   Upper class

Rethinking in Context: How much social mobility has occurred in your family in the last three generations? In what ways did the social structure and economic system contribute to the mobility or lack thereof? Is upward mobility more difficult now or in the time of your great-grandparents? Why? Do you know any married couples whose social-class backgrounds were quite different from each other? Is this a problem in their marriages?

Multiple Choice Questions

1.   A society in which there is no social mobility is called a(n)
     a.   Open system
     b.   Closed system
     c.   Meritocracy
     d.   Ascription

2.   A society in which the status of one's parents has no influence on one's own status is called
     a.   Closed
     b.   Open
     c.   Bounded
     d.   Status by ascription

3.   According to Marx, hunting-gathering societies were characterized by
     a.   Socialism
     b.   Primitive communism
     c.   Nobility
     d.   Existentialism

4.   Contemporary conflict theorists suggest
     a.   Stratification can be destructive to society as a whole
     b.   Stratification systems are unfair
     c.   Stratification systems tend to be exploitive of the "have-nots"
     d.   All of the above

5.	Functionalism argues that stratification is
	a.	Necessary for societies to survive
	b.	Needed so rich people can grow richer
	c.	Found only in postindustrial societies
	d.	None of the above

6.	One characteristic of a "culture of poverty" is
	a.	Delayed gratification
	b.	Immediate gratification
	c.	Blaming the victim
	d.	A strongly individualistic ethos

7.	Statements such as "children who grow up in working-class families tend to be working class themselves" illustrate
	a.	Cultural capital
	b.	Social reproduction
	c.	Meritocracy
	d.	Weber's theory

8.	Weber thought that social inequality was based on
	a.	Wealth
	b.	Power
	c.	Prestige
	d.	All of the above

9.	"Status borrowing" is a concept that is relevant in discussions concerning
	a.	Education
	b.	Occupational prestige
	c.	Marital satisfaction
	d.	Religious differences

10.	What has more impact on a child's college success chances?
	a.	Mother's education
	b.	Father's education
	c.	Grandparent's education
	d.	Sibling's education

11.	Poverty rates for Black children in the 1990s
	a.	Increased
	b.	Decreased
	c.	Stayed the same

12.   The family form more likely to be poor is
        a.   A single male-headed household
        b.   A single female-headed household
        c.   Grandparents raising grandchildren
        d.   Two-parent working families

13.   Sweden has a high unwed pregnancy rate and
        a.   Most unwed mothers are poor
        b.   There is relatively little poverty
        c.   Fathers rarely live in the household
        d.   None of the above

14.   In the United States, teenage mothers are
        a.   Less likely to finish high school
        b.   More likely to get and keep well-paying jobs
        c.   Less likely to live in poverty for long periods of time
        d.   All of the above

15.   The group of workers more vulnerable to a country's economic health are
        a.   Upper-middle-class professionals
        b.   Middle-class clerical workers
        c.   Blue collar or working class
        d.   Retirees

16.   A person who comes into more contact with others who have a diversity of experiences is more likely to have a(n)
        a.   Restricted code
        b.   Elaborated code
        c.   Nonexistent linguistic code
        d.   Perpetual code

17.   An example characteristic of a restricted code would be
        a.   Strong punishments for deviation from the norm
        b.   Liberal political beliefs
        c.   Tolerance of differences
        d.   Permissive styles of discipline

18.   A member of which class would be more likely to see work as intrinsically rewarding?
        a.   Working class
        b.   Poor
        c.   Upper-middle class
        d.   Wealthy class

19.   Social insulation would be more characteristic of the
      a.   Middle class
      b.   Upper class
      c.   Working class
      d.   Poor

20.   The class most likely to be more politically active would be the
      a.   Upper class
      b.   Middle class
      c.   Working class
      d.   Poor

True/False

1.   Meritocracies can be found in many countries today.
2.   Marx believed workers and owners would/should become the same people.
3.   Davis and Moore believed social stratification was necessary to society.
4.   Cultural capital is the same as money.
5.   Weber had a one-dimensional model of social classification.
6.   Occupational prestige has changed drastically over the last fifty years.
7.   The social class of one's parents, especially their educational level, is a strong predictor for one's success in school.
8.   In the United States, poverty is a permanent condition for many people.
9.   Nearly half of children live in poverty in the United States.
10. Working-class couples tend to wait to have their first child because of economic pressures.

Matching

The terms introduced in this chapter are listed here in alphabetical order. Match the terms with the appropriate definition.

_____	1	Ascription	A	An ideal-typical system of social stratification in which there is no mobility; all status is by ascription.
_____	2	Bourgeoisie	B	An annual income amount that separates the poor from the nonpoor.
_____	3	Closed mobility system	C	An ideal-typical system of social stratification in which there is total mobility; all status is by achievement.
_____	4	Cultural capital	D	Assignment to a position because of characteristics, such as race, sex, or family ancestry, over which the individual has no control.
_____	5	Feminization of poverty	E	Government by persons found to be most capable.

	6	Meritocracy	F	Redistribution of something of value from one person or group to another person or group, not based on work the receiver is performing.
	7	Open mobility system	G	Respect or favorable regard attached to a person because of his or her position in the social system.
	8	Poverty threshold	H	The general cultural background, knowledge, disposition, and skills that are passed from one generation to the next.
	9	Prestige	I	The impression that women are increasingly likely to be poor because of the increasing concentration of poverty in female-headed families.
	10	Proletariat	J	The probability of controlling or influencing the behavior of other persons, even against resistance.
	11	Social power	K	The process whereby a society reproduces its system of inequality from one generation to the next.
	12	Social reproduction	L	The social class that, in Marxist theory, controls the means of production and uses capital, natural resources, and exploited labor to make profits.
	13	Transfer payments	M	The social class that, in Marxist theory, labors as the instrument of production for the bourgeoisie.
	14	Trickle-down economics	N	The view that directly helping the poor will create a demand for goods and services that will improve the economy.
	15	Trickle-up economics	O	The view that increased wealth in the hands of the rich will result in an improved economy that will help the poor.

Short Essay

1. Discuss why it seems easy to "blame the victims" of poverty, including some of the common stereotypes.
2. Contrast Marx's and Weber's theories of social stratification.
3. Discuss the concept of "feminization of poverty."

Critical Thinking

1. Consider a proposal to eliminate all inheritance tax in the United States and to make people at all income levels pay the same percentage in income taxes (i.e., get rid of the graduated income tax wherein those with higher incomes pay a higher rate of tax). Discuss how a conflict theorist and a functionalist might analyze this proposal.
2. Discuss whether or not you think a truly classless society is possible or would work. Support your position with specific examples.

3. Social reproduction occurs, among other places, in the family institution. If the United States were to attempt to make life fairer by eliminating social reproduction, what changes would have to occur in the family?

Additional Small Group Discussions

Construct a list of "reasons for poverty." For each of these reasons, discuss whether it is best explained with a structural-conflict, a structural-functional, cultural, or individual theoretical perspective. What are the political implications of each "reason"?

Answer Keys

Multiple Choice

1.	b	6.	b	11.	b	16.	b
2.	b	7.	b	12.	b	17.	a
3.	b	8.	d	13.	b	18.	c
4.	d	9.	b	14.	a	19.	b
5.	a	10.	a	15.	c	20.	a

True/False

1.	f	6.	f
2.	t	7.	t
3.	t	8.	f
4.	f	9.	f
5.	f	10.	f

Matching

1.	D	9.	G
2.	L	10.	M
3.	A	11.	J
4.	H	12.	K
5.	I	13.	F
6.	E	14.	O
7.	C	15.	N
8.	B		

Short Essay

1. Discuss why it seems easy to "blame the victims" of poverty, including some of the common stereotypes.
   a. Poor people are lazy, lack self-control, talent or ability, and have substance-abuse problems
   b. No good measures for these characteristics
   c. Cycles of intergenerational poverty
   d. Issues of human capital

2. Contrast Marx's and Weber's theories of social stratification.
   a. Marx—one dimensional; thought main tension was between ruling and working class
   b. Weber—multidimensional; thought wealth, power, and prestige interacted to form class positions

3. Discuss the concept of "feminization of poverty."
   a. Based on increase in single female-headed households
   b. Rates of unwed births contribute to this impression as well
   c. Relates to earnings gap discussion

Chapter 7 Race/Ethnicity and Families

Learning Objectives

After reading this chapter, you should be able to
1. Describe the differences between the concepts of race and ethnicity.
2. Discuss how immigration patterns have influenced changing attitudes about race.
3. Explain how fertility rates relate to the discussion of immigration and ethnicity.
4. Define and provide an example of acculturation.
5. Outline social class patterns and trends in relation to immigration influences.
6. Describe several key characteristics of impacts on Native American families, African American families, Hispanic families and Asian American families.
7. Discuss social class in relation to Black working-class families.
8. Describe diversity in terms of White Americans, using Irish American and Italian American families as examples.
9. Discuss how race and ethnicity are socially constructed and will change with societal changes.

Chapter Outline

Thinking Ahead: Are you more likely to be good friends with someone who is the same race as yourself but of a very different class, or someone who is the same class but a different race? Which are you most likely to live next door to? To marry? Why? What advantages or disadvantages, if any, have you experienced because of your race or ethnicity?

1) What is Race and Ethnicity?

2) Categorizing "Race" and "Ethnicity"

3) Race/Ethnicity in America's Past and Future
   a) Immigration and changing diversity
   b) Race/ethnicity, social class, and family

4) Native American Families

5) The Family among African Americans
   a) Changing terminology
   b) African Americans since slavery
   c) Family instability, poverty, and society
   d) Working-class and affluent Black families

6) Hispanic Families in the United States
   a) Hispanic diversity
   b) Mexican American families

7) Asian American Families
    a)   Asian American diversity
    b)   Japanese Americans

8) White Americans and the Family
    a)   European American Diversity
        i)   Irish Americans
        ii) Italian Americans

Rethinking in Context: Are class-related or race-related variables better predictors of family life? If interracial marriages become more common, how would that affect the concept of race and ethnicity? Have you changed your view of the advantages and disadvantages of your race/ethnicity? Which groups have been most advantaged? Least advantaged? How have families affected these differences?

Multiple Choice Questions

1.   The concept of "race" was developed by
        a.   Hitler
        b.   The science of genetics and theories of evolution
        c.   The royalty in Britain
        d.   Seventeenth century Americans

2.   Ethnicity, as a concept, is determined by one's
        a.   Genetic makeup
        b.   Current location or geographic region
        c.   Identification with a particular group
        d.   Both (b) and (c) above

3.   When the U.S. economy is good, immigration generally
        a.   Increases
        b.   Decreases
        c.   Remains the same

4.   Until the middle of the twentieth century most immigrants to the United States came from
        a.   Latin America
        b.   Asian countries
        c.   European countries
        d.   Russia

5.   Which group of Americans tends to have the highest fertility rates?
    a.   African Americans
    b.   Hispanic Americans
    c.   Asian Americans
    d.   Native Americans

6.   Which group is most likely to have the highest median income level?
    a.   Blacks
    b.   Whites
    c.   Asians
    d.   Hispanics

7.   Which group of young Americans is most likely to attend college?
    a.   Blacks
    b.   Whites
    c.   Hispanics
    d.   Asians

8.   The category of Native Americans who are people attempting to redefine and reconfirm cultural styles are called
    a.   Traditionalists
    b.   Bicultural
    c.   Pan-traditional
    d.   Pagans

9.   During the early part of the 1900s, many young Black men migrated north primarily to
    a.   Find marriage partners
    b.   Obtain manufacturing jobs
    c.   Escape racism and inequality in the South
    d.   All of the above

10.   Black women who migrated north were most likely to be employed in
    a.   Manufacturing jobs
    b.   Domestic work
    c.   Agricultural jobs
    d.   The clothing industry

11.   The concept of family sharing is more closely associated with
    a.   Black families
    b.   White families
    c.   Income level
    d.   None of the above

12. The Moynihan report was criticized because it said
    a. The Black family was adaptive and resilient
    b. The Black family was a cause of poverty, crime, and other social problems
    c. Black families have too many children out of wedlock
    d. Black families are stable

13. Wilson wrote several books suggesting
    a. There is more similarity between Blacks and Whites than originally thought
    b. Poverty is the common denominator rather than race
    c. Prejudice and discrimination are less important than social class
    d. All of the above

14. Working-class Black families
    a. Are not very much like working-class White families
    b. Often have college educations
    c. Have nontraditional role expectations about housework
    d. Are quite similar to working-class White families

15. Middle-class Black families are likely to
    a. Have the most egalitarian marriages of any group
    b. Have some college education and strongly encourage their children to go to college
    c. Grow up in intact families
    d. All of the above

16. The group within the Hispanic category most likely to be living in poverty are
    a. Cuban Americans
    b. Mexican Americans
    c. Puerto Ricans
    d. Latin Americans

17. The group most likely to use extended kin for support are
    a. African Americans
    b. Chicanos
    c. Anglos
    d. Asian Americans

18. The group within Asian Americans most likely to be experiencing poverty would be from
    a. Japan
    b. China
    c. Korea
    d. Southeast Asia

19.   The group most likely to have the highest levels of education is
        a.   German immigrants
        b.   Jews from Eastern Europe
        c.   WASPs (White Anglo-Saxon Protestants)
        d.   Hispanics

20.   Similarities between Irish American families and Italian American families include
        a.   Creating strong families and ethnic enclaves
        b.   Suffering prejudice in the United States
        c.   Coming from wealthy backgrounds
        d.   Both (a) and (b) above

True/False

1.   It is easy to classify people into one ethnic category.
2.   Religion is unrelated to discussions of race and ethnicity.
3.   Voluntary immigrants have fared much better historically than involuntary immigrants in the United States.
4.   Most Americans today think Jewish people make up about 18% of the population when in fact they constitute between 2-3%.
5.   By 2050, Non-Hispanic Whites will become a minority in the United States.
6.   Hispanics are more likely to have more prestigious blue-collar jobs than other groups.
7.   Whites and Blacks are more likely to live alone than Hispanics, Asians, or Native Americans.
8.   There is no history of nuclear families among African Americans.
9.   Blacks who are in the upper class are more likely to have a "patriarchal affluent" family pattern.
10. Familism is most characteristic of White families.
11. Japanese Americans suffered no discrimination during WWII.
12. Many Japanese American families place emphasis on parent-child units rather than husband-wife dyads.
13. Italian families had little difficulty assimilating into American cities.

Matching

The terms introduced in this chapter are listed here in alphabetical order. Match the terms with the appropriate definition.

_____   1   Acculturation   A   A traditional Mexican custom of co-parenthood that developed from God-parenthood.

_____   2   Braceros   B   Group distinction based on national origin or distinctive cultural patterns such as religion, language, or region.

_____   3   Chicanos   C   A group defined by socially selected physical characteristics.

	4	Compadrazgo	D	Alternative name for Mexican-Americans.
____	5	Emigration	E	First-generation Japanese immigrants to the United States, mostly between 1890 and 1920.
____	6	Ethnicity	F	House, immediate family, household.
____	7	Fertility rate	G	Ideal-typical characteristics of manliness in a highly differentiated Mexican or Mexican American gender role structure.
____	8	Immigration	H	Movement *into* a non-native country or region.
____	9	Issei	I	Movement *out of* a native country or region.
____	10	La Casa	J	Process by which immigrant groups assimilate into a dominant or host culture and change their values, language and practices.
____	11	Machismo	K	Second-generation Japanese-Americans, mostly born between 1910 and 1940.
____	12	Nisei	L	The total number of children each woman is expected to have over a lifetime.
____	13	Race	M	Third-generation Japanese Americans, mostly born after World War II.
____	14	Sansei	N	Workers who are expected to return to Mexico after a temporary period of employment.

Short Essay

1. Discuss what contributions "fictive" kin may make to family structures.
2. Describe Wilson's idea about the "culture of poverty." What is his solution to the "blaming the victim" argument?
3. Discuss how "familism" works in Chicano families.

Critical Thinking

1. Discuss the controversies surrounding bilingual education. Use at least one outside resource to clarify your argument. Which stance would you take if you were a legislator faced with making these decisions? How does access to education impact family function, particularly with immigrant families?

2. Describe your experiences of "fictive kin" or "family of choice." Whom do you consider to be "family" even if they are not actually related to you by blood or marriage? How do race/ethnicity class, gender, and generation impact those relationships? You may wish to consider constructing a "family of choice" genogram to compare with your "family of origin" genogram.

3. Which do you think has a bigger impact on individuals' life chances—social class or race/ethnicity? Support your position with data and logic.

Additional Small Group Discussions

Suppose your small group has been assigned the task by the Census Bureau of designing the items on the next census that will be used to determine each person's "race" or "ethnicity." Each person in the country will be asked to check their race and ethnicity from the form you develop. Each person must have one—and only one—option to check in each category of race and ethnicity. If the two categories are combined, each person must have only one option in the combined category.

What would be the consequences if the race and ethnicity questions were simply omitted from the census? (Remember that the Census Bureau provides much of this country's information about income, educational level, type of residence, and so on, by race and ethnicity.)

Answer Keys

Multiple Choice

1.	b	7.	d	13.	d	19.	b
2.	d	8.	c	14.	d	20.	d
3.	a	9.	b	15.	d		
4.	c	10.	b	16.	c		
5.	b	11.	c	17.	b		
6.	c	12.	b	18.	d		

True/False

1.	f		8.	f
2.	f		9.	t
3.	t		10.	f
4.	t		11.	f
5.	f		12.	t
6.	t		13.	t
7.	t			

Matching

1.	J		8.	H
2.	N		9.	E
3.	D		10.	F
4.	A		11.	G
5.	I		12.	K
6.	B		13.	C
7.	L		14.	M

Short Essay

1. Discuss what contributions "fictive" kin may make to family structures.
   a. Creates more fluid households
   b. More role sharing and caretaker responsibilities
   c. May be characteristic of resource sharing when people live in poverty

2. Describe Wilson's idea about the "culture of poverty." What is his solution to the "blaming the victim" argument?
   a. Wilson says the culture will exist only as long as the conditions, such as joblessness, continue to exist
   b. The culture of poverty perpetuates development of an "underclass" that can be supported intergenerationally

3. Discuss how "familism" works in Chicano families.
   a. Interest of individuals are surpassed by interests of groups
   b. La Casa example
   c. Resource sharing, especially financial assistance
   d. Shared living arrangements

Chapter 8 Forming Intimate Relationships

Learning Objectives

After reading this chapter, you should be able to
1. Place love into a historical context and understand that romantic love is a relatively recent concept.
2. Discuss how love can be defined and the complexities of measuring such a concept.
3. Outline the characteristics of Lee's typology of love.
4. Describe other theories of love, including Sternberg's triangle theory, Reiss's wheel of love, and Murstein's sequential state theory.
5. Understand how several key sociological theories might explain love.
6. Discuss how society has "feminized" love and how men and women have been socialized to view love differently.
7. Describe sociobiological theories and sexual strategies approaches to mate selection.
8. Explain patterns of breakups in relationships and briefly outline the research on dating violence.

Chapter Outline

Thinking Ahead: Make a list of the characteristics that would attract you to a member of the opposite sex; make another list of those characteristics that you would find desirable in a close same-sex friendship. How do the lists compare? How do you think your lists would compare with the lists made by someone of the opposite sex?

1) Historical Images of Love
   a) Is love universal?
   b) Love in Ancient Greece and Rome
   c) Courtly love in Europe
   d) Romanticism and industrialization

2) Defining Love
   a) Descriptive variation in defining love
   b) Love as a symbol

3) Typologies of Love

4) Lee's love styles
   a) Research with Lee's typology
   b) Passion, companionship, and commitment
   c) Sociological viewpoints on love
       i)   Symbolic interactionism
       ii) Conflict theory
       iii) Structure-functionalism

5) Process of Love
   a) Individualistic compatibility theories
      i) Parental image theories
      ii) Complementary needs
   b) Value and role compatibility
      i) Value theories
      ii) Role consensus
   c) Sequential stage theories
      i) The wheel theory of love
      ii) The stimulus-value-role (SVR) model

6) Gender Differences in Love
   a) Feminization of love
   b) Male and female loving styles

7) Sexual Strategies Theory

8) Breakdowns and Breakups
   a) Relationship risks and strengths
   b) Jealousy
   c) Dating violence

Rethinking in Context: Reconsider the list of attractive characteristics you made before reading the chapter. Did your list correspond with the gender expectation suggested in the chapter? Were the characteristics you desired more compatible with short-term or long-term mating selection? What process of developing intimacy does your list imply?

Multiple Choice Questions

1. Love, as described by Plato, in Greek society, had which of the following characteristics?
    a. A spiritual quest for truth and beauty
    b. Strongly committed monogamous relationships
    c. No evidence of homosexuality
    d. Little evidence of passionate love

2. Which of the following traits would be consistent with courtly love?
    a. Spiritual love for God
    b. Passionate heterosexual attraction
    c. Loyalty of servant to master
    d. All of the above

3. "Romantic" love would justify which of the following?
   a. Revolt against authority
   b. Individualism
   c. Cultivation of emotion
   d. All of the above

4. In "love-appropriate" relationships, the word "love" can occur in
   a. Predictable ways
   b. Ritualistic fashion
   c. Reciprocal circumstances
   d. All of the above

5. John feels intense passion, including physical and sexual attraction, for Sally. He is quite willing to tell her everything and is certain she is the "love of his life." John is exhibiting which of Lee's love styles?
   a. Storge
   b. Eros
   c. Pragma
   d. Mania

6. Samantha is quite interested in Kelly because she thinks Kelly's income will be stable and reliable. They seem to get along well, although there is no intense attraction or passion present. Which of Lee's love styles is Samantha exhibiting?
   a. Ludus
   b. Mania
   c. Pragma
   d. Agape

7. Jesse is certain that Justin is cheating on her when he is out of town. This makes her feel very depressed and jealous and she has even thought of suicide upon occasion. Which of Lee's love styles is Jesse most like?
   a. Agape
   b. Ludus
   c. Mania
   d. Storge

8. Research done using Lee's typology suggests
   a. There is no difference in love styles based on ethnicity
   b. Religiosity is irrelevant to love styles
   c. Partners in relationships tend to have similar love styles
   d. Couples who were high on Ludus were most likely to stay together

9. John Money's "love blot" concept suggests
   a. Individuals have images that they project onto another person about what an ideal lover should be like
   b. Creating ideal images of a romantic partner is part of the process most people go through and is a reliable basis for forming relationships
   c. Love can be predicted by using tests like Rorschach's inkblot tests
   d. None of the above

10. The three components of Sternberg's theory are
    a. Physical arousal, passion, commitment
    b. Emotional component, intimacy, passion
    c. Passion, commitment, intimacy
    d. Consummate love, intimacy, passion

11. Which sociological theory would view love as the "glue that holds families and communities together"?
    a. Conflict-feminist
    b. Symbolic interaction
    c. Structure-functionalism
    d. Sociobiological

12. Most of the parental image theories, concepts, and ideas have descended from
    a. B. F. Skinner
    b. Sigmund Freud
    c. George Herbert Mead
    d. Ira Reiss

13. Complementary needs theory suggests
    a. People seek partners who have the same needs as they do
    b. People look for partners who will help meet their psychological needs
    c. Dominance and submission are irrelevant in this theory
    d. None of the above

14. Value theories suggest that people are attracted to those
    a. They perceive as more valuable than themselves
    b. Who have dissimilar values
    c. Who have similar values
    d. All of the above

15. The four spokes of Reiss's wheel of love theory are
    a. Rapport, self-revelation, intimacy-need fulfillment, mutual dependence
    b. Mutual dependence, passion, commitment, intimacy-need fulfillment
    c. Intimacy, rapport, self-revelation, commitment
    d. Passion, rapport, mutual dependence, intimacy

16. An example of an "open field" situation, according to Murstein's stimulus value theory, is a
    a. Boss/worker relationship
    b. Student in the same sociology class
    c. Co-worker
    d. Teacher/student relationship

17. The three components of Murstein's theory are
    a. Stimulus, value comparison, roles
    b. Suggestion, values, rapport
    c. Passion, intimacy, commitment
    d. Values, stimulus, rapport

18. The "sexual strategies" theory suggests
    a. Men want to be monogamous
    b. Women should engage in short-term mating
    c. Women are more likely to have greater payoffs from long-term mating
    d. Men are not interested in short-term mating

19. Which of the following characteristics is most likely to contribute to relationship breakdowns?
    a. Differences in religious faith
    b. Parental disapproval
    c. Differences in leisure time activities
    d. Age differences

20. In terms of dating violence, research has suggested that
    a. One partner is usually the perpetrator and the other the victim
    b. Both partners use the same types of violence
    c. Both partners tend to be both aggressors and victims
    d. None of the above

True/False

1. Several anthropologists have suggested that romantic love is a characteristic of human groups, even in hunting-gathering societies.
2. Troubadours were traveling storytellers who spread tales of courtly love.

3. The English language has an extensive vocabulary for naming various types of love.
4. According to Sternberg's triangle love theory, couples who have similar love triangles will feel much excitement or happiness in their relationship.
5. One of the critiques about the "feminization of love" suggests that the measurements of love do not adequately measure instrumental and sexual expressions of love.
6. Some researchers suggest that women move more slowly into romantic relationships because they have more at risk.
7. The example of Chinese arranged marriages has been used to illustrate conflict/feminist theory.
8. Women tend to think sexual infidelity is more distressing than emotional infidelity.
9. Men tend to initiate breakups more often than women.

Matching

The terms introduced in this chapter are listed here in alphabetical order. Match the terms with the appropriate definition.

_____	1	Agape	A	A code of romantic behavior idealized among the aristocracy of medieval Europe.
_____	2	Courtly love	B	An affiliation in which the partners mutually accept the use of the word "love."
_____	3	Eros	C	The something else for which a symbol stands.
_____	4	Love contract	D	A scientific approach that attempts to use biological and evolutionary principles to explain the behavior of all social animals, including human beings.
_____	5	Love-appropriate relationship	E	A systematic classification of related phenomena based on defined characteristics or traits.
_____	6	Ludus	F	A thing that stands for something else.
_____	7	Mania	G	Affectionate, companionate style of loving.
_____	8	Pragma	H	An artistic and intellectual movement originating in Europe in the late 18th century.
_____	9	Principle of least interest	I	Expectations partners in a love-appropriate relationship have for each other and themselves.
_____	10	Referent	J	Idea that the partner who cares the least about the relationship has the most power.
_____	11	Romanticism	K	Love as play and recreation.
_____	12	Sociobiology	L	Love style characterized by nurturing concern and self-sacrifice.
_____	13	Storge	M	Love style emphasizing practical elements in relationships and rationality in partner selection.

| ____ | 14 | Symbol | N | Love style with intense emotional and sexual attachment, but without possessiveness. |
| ____ | 15 | Typology | O | Love style with strong emotional intensity, sexual attraction, jealousy, and moodiness. |

Short Essay

1. Discuss how the world "love" is most often used as a symbol. Be sure to include examples of referents.
2. Discuss Cancian's ideas on the "feminization of love" with respect to gender differences.
3. Support or refute sociobiological theories of mate selection. Include several examples to illustrate your perspective.

Critical Thinking

1. Select a current movie of your choice that depicts at least one romantic relationship. Discuss the film in terms of one of the theories presented in this chapter. Be sure to use specific examples from the film to demonstrate that you understand the theory.
2. Investigate some of the historical contexts for "love" on the Internet. There is an extensive list of links to begin with at "Resources for Love & Spirituality East & West" (http://home.sandiego.edu/~lnelson/love.shtml). Compare and contrast at least two different religious perspectives on love.
3. Critique some of the "love tests" found at sites like "Free Love Tests, Love Quizzes, Online Love Test, Love Quiz, Relationship Help" (http:www.links2love.com/quizzes_love.htm) and compare them to the Love Attitudes Scales discussed in your text. How might you determine which is more reliable?

Additional Small Group Discussions

In the 1950s and 1960s, couples had a "continuum of closeness" from stranger to married: having a date; dating; going steady; engaged; married. Most steps were indicated with a symbol of some kind, such as a class ring, engagement ring, etc. Couples knew what relationship term to call each other when introductions were made to other people: "This is my girlfriend/boyfriend," or "this is my fiancée" or "this is my wife/husband."

Your discussion task is to construct a continuum for your generation. Place the following terms, and any others that might seem relevant, on the continuum: seeing; married; engaged; going with; dating; going out with; cohabiting; getting together; etc. Place them in proper order on the "continuum of closeness":

Stranger_____Spouse

For each term, indicate the couple's expectations about such matters as exclusivity of the relationship. Is there a symbol associated with the term? Does the couple talk about what stage they are in? If not, how do they know they are both at that same stage? What term would one member of the couple use to introduce the other to some third person such as an old friend? At what stage is sexual intercourse typically included, according to the norms of your closest friends?

Answer Keys

Multiple Choice

1.	a	6.	c	11.	c	16.	b
2.	d	7.	c	12.	b	17.	a
3.	d	8.	c	13.	b	18.	c
4.	d	9.	a	14.	c	19.	c
5.	b	10.	c	15.	a	20.	c

True/False

1.	t	6.	t
2.	t	7.	f
3.	f	8.	f
4.	t	9.	f
5.	t		

Matching

1.	L	9.	J
2.	A	10.	C
3.	N	11.	H
4.	I	12.	D
5.	B	13.	G
6.	K	14.	F
7.	O	15.	E
8.	M		

Short Essay

1. Discuss how the world "love" is most often used as a symbol. Be sure to include examples of referents.
    a. Symbols are arbitrary and learned
    b. Symbols refer to emotions and feelings
    c. Symbol "love" may be associated with behavioral expectations
    d. Expressing love can become ritualistic
    e. Expression of love can become reciprocal

2. Discuss Cancian's ideas on the "feminization of love" with respect to gender differences.
    a. Historical context of industrialization
    b. "Cult of domesticity" and association of women with emotional work
    c. Chodorow and psychoanalytic view suggests men less capable of love
    d. Measurement issues

3. Support or refute sociobiological theories of mate selection. Include several examples to illustrate your perspective.
    a. Pro: two examples provided in text of kibbutzim and Chinese arranged marriages
    b. Con: if purpose is to "propagate the species," how do we explain same-sex relationships?

Chapter 9 Mate Selection

Learning Objectives

After reading this chapter, you should be able to
1. Briefly discuss changes in mate selection historically.
2. Explain why the split between work and home was significant in terms of mate selection.
3. Discuss formal versus informal dating patterns.
4. Outline the characteristics of social exchange theory in terms of mate selection.
5. Describe key factors of single life and cohabitation.
6. Compare homosexual relationships with heterosexual patterns of mate selection.
7. Discuss the key variables or traits that most people assess when selecting a mate.

Chapter Outline

Thinking Ahead: Suppose you run an agency whose task it is to select mates for customers. You get paid when a couple you arrange gets married, plus an annual fee for each year the marriage lasts. What kinds of characteristics are you going to look for in matching your couples? How will you decide which individuals to introduce to each other?

1) History of Mate Selection
    a)   The mate selection continuum
    b)   Preindustrial mate selection
    c)   Courtship in industrial America
        i)   Phase 1
        ii)   Phase 2
        iii) Phase 3
        iv) Phase 4

2) Courtship in Postindustrial America
    a)   Getting together
    b)   The selection process
        i)   Social exchange theory
        ii)   New rational partner selection
    c)   Class and race differences

3) Homogamy in mate selection
    a)   Racial homogamy
    b)   Religious homogamy
    c)   Social class homogamy
    d)   Theories about class homogamy
        i)   Social exchange theory
        ii)   Equity theory

        iii) Functionalism
        iv) Conflict theory
        v) Symbolic interactionism
  e) Propinquity
  f) Age hypergamy and the marriage squeeze

4) The singles option
  a) Singlehood in perspective
  b) Cohabitation
        i) Cohabiting and the unmarried couple household
        ii) Demographics of cohabiting
        iii) Life among cohabitants
  c) Marriage and single life compared
  d) Gay and lesbian relationships

Rethinking in Context: Consider the criteria you used in matching your prospective couples. Based on what you found out in this chapter, would you make any changes? Considering the importance of homogamy in mate selection, did you include matching by social class, race, religion, and age? If you were actually running a matching business, would this be considered a discriminatory practice according to federal civil right laws? Would your request payment if the couple moved in together rather than getting married?

Multiple Choice Questions

1.   Shinyo's marriage was arranged by his aunt and his future bride's cousin. This type of relationship would be classified as _____ on Adam's mate selection continuum
      a. Completely controlled
      b. Restricted choice
      c. Universal permanent availability
      d. Random

2.   Mr. and Mrs. Smith would really like their daughter to marry an Ivy League graduate. With that agenda in mind, they have sent her to college at Wellesley, an elite women's college. If her future partner came from nearby Harvard or other Ivy League institution, this type of relationship would be classified as
      a. Complete controlled choice
      b. Restricted choice
      c. Universal permanent availability
      d. Random

3. Hunting-gathering societies tended to be at which end of Adams's mate selection continuum?
    a. Completely controlled choice
    b. Restricted choice
    c. Universal permanent availability
    d. Random

4. During Phase 1 of industrialized America, courtship between a young man and woman usually began by the
    a. Young man asking the young woman out on a date
    b. Young woman telling her friends she was interested in the young man
    c. Young woman's mother issuing an invitation to the young man
    d. Couple meeting at a social event or church function

5. The custom of "dating" was started during
    a. Phase 1
    b. Phase 2
    c. Phase 3
    d. Phase 4

6. During the 1950s, which of the following was not typically part of the dating process?
    a. Going steady
    b. Marrying for romantic love
    c. Engagement
    d. Cohabitation

7. Which of the following is not one of Sprecher and Mett's characterizations of romantic ideals?
    a. Love at first sight
    b. Love conquers all
    c. True love is absolutely perfect
    d. We should choose partners for practical reasons

8. In terms of age differences between the groom and bride, which of the following is most true?
    a. There was a narrow age gap in the late 1800s
    b. The age gap is wider now than ever before
    c. The age gap has narrowed consistently with time
    d. Brides now are slightly older than their grooms

9. Most people will have _____ in terms of general marital desirability ratings
    a. Large differences
    b. Small differences
    c. Similar scores
    d. None of the above

10. The pool of eligibles in agricultural societies was _____ than it is today
    a. similar
    b. larger
    c. smaller
    d. no different

11. Men who use "mail order bride" services tend to be
    a. Disillusioned with American women
    b. Young and inexperienced
    c. Looking for equal partnerships
    d. All of the above

12. Formal engagements would be more likely among _____ classes
    a. Lower
    b. Upper
    c. Middle
    d. No differences

13. Which category of people would statistically be most likely to marry outside their race?
    a. White men
    b. Black women
    c. Native American women
    d. Japanese American men

14. Which factor have some researchers discovered is more important than religious homogamy?
    a. Social class
    b. Education
    c. Physical appearance
    d. Race

15. The idea that people with more resources are able to bargain for more resources in their spouses reflects
    a. Conflict theory
    b. Social exchange theory
    c. Feminist theory
    d. Functionalism

16.   Patrick comes from a wealthy family and has become engaged to Janelle, who is also
        from a wealthy family. Which theory would support the notion that this union will
        increase wealth and power and prevent it from being dispersed to the lower classes?
        a.   Conflict theory
        b.   Social exchange theory
        c.   Equity theory
        d.   Functionalism

17.   People who meet over the Internet and have very little face-to-face contact with each
        other refute which of the following concepts?
        a.   Equity theory
        b.   Social exchange theory
        c.   Propinquity
        d.   Functionalism

18.   The marriage squeeze for women can be caused by
        a.   Age hypergamy
        b.   Age homogamy
        c.   Low death rates for men
        d.   None of the above

19.   The rate of people who have never married historically has
        a.   Changed drastically
        b.   Changed very little
        c.   No data available

20.   According to a study done by Casper and Sayer, most people who are cohabiting
        classified their relationship as
        a.   A substitution for marriage
        b.   A precursor for marriage
        c.   A trial marriage
        d.   Co-residential dating

21.   Married couples tend to fare better than cohabiting couples on which of the following?
        a.   Physical and mental health
        b.   Labor productivity
        c.   Life expectancy
        d.   All of the above

22.   Jessie Bernard found that single women report _____
       a.   More nervousness, insomnia, nightmares and headaches
       b.   Fewer symptoms of mental illness
       c.   Better health in general
       d.   All of the above

23.   Which is most true of gay and lesbian relationships?
       a.   Gay men and lesbians look for the same qualities in relationships as do
            heterosexual men and women
       b.   Rates of breakups are vastly different from heterosexual cohabiting ones
       c.   There is no difference in personal ads between homosexual and heterosexual
            people
       d.   None of the above

True/False

1.   During the Victorian era there was less emphasis placed on formal courtship and sexual
     mores.
2.   Courtship trends in post-industrial America (current day) have moved toward the open-
     choice side of the mate-selection continuum.
3.   Average age at first marriage is currently lower than at any other time in history.
4.   Mail-order brides are almost unheard of in today's marriage marketplace.
5.   Poor people tend to have less formal patterns for dating and mate selection.
6.   Successful marriages tend to be heterogamous.
7.   It is more common for both men and women to engage in hypergamy than hypogamy.
8.   Worldwide the average age gap between men and women in marriage is three years.
9.   Today younger people are more likely to cohabit than were younger people thirty years ago.
10. In Sweden, where there is a high rate of cohabitation, people who cohabitated eight years or
     more before marriage were likely to divorce.

Matching

The terms introduced in this chapter are listed here in alphabetical order. Match the terms with the
appropriate definition.

_____	1	Arranged marriage	A	A demographic condition in which there are considerably more eligible mates for one sex than for another.
_____	2	Assortive mating	B	Formal norms against marriage of persons of different races.
_____	3	Bachelor	C	Living together, especially as an intimate couple in a marriage-like relationship.
_____	4	Cohabiting	D	Nearness; the tendency to select mates from persons who live nearby.
_____	5	Endogamy	E	A set of norms that specify whom a person should marry.

_____	6	Exogamy	F	A social condition wherein any individual is always a potential mate for anyone else.
_____	7	General marital desirability	G	A value system emphasizing a strong sense of duty and strict sexual morality: after Queen Victoria of England.
_____	8	Heterogamy	H	A woman who remains unmarried beyond the typical marriage age.
_____	9	Homogamy	I	An unmarried girl or woman, usually assumed to be a virgin.
_____	10	Hypergamy	J	An unmarried man.
_____	11	Hypogamy	K	Marriage between individuals with characteristics that society generally defines as grounds for homogamy.
_____	12	Maiden	L	Marriage in which the woman marries into a higher social level.
_____	13	Marriage market	M	Marriage in which the woman marries into a lower social level.
_____	14	Marriage squeeze	N	Marriage with a person of lower social position.
_____	15	Mating gradient	O	Mate selection by someone other than the potential mates.
_____	16	Mésalliance	P	Mate selection from outside the group.
_____	17	Miscegenation laws	Q	Mate selection from within the group.
_____	18	Mixed marriage rate for individuals	R	Result of a tendency to have more hypergamy than hypogamy in a mate-selection system.
_____	19	Mixed marriage	S	Selection of mates from among those with different social characteristics.
_____	20	Mixed marriages rate	T	Selection of mates from those with similar social characteristics.
_____	21	Person-specific marital desirability	U	The concept that individuals or their families shop and bargain for mates in a way similar to economic transactions.
_____	22	Pool of eligibles	V	The desirability of a person as a mate based on another individual's particular preferences.
_____	23	Prescriptive mating system	W	The desirability of a person as a mate based on socially agreed-upon resources.
_____	24	Propinquity	X	The group of individuals constituting realistic potential mates.

	25	Spinster	Y	The percent of individuals of a particular group who are married to an individual who is not in the group in question.
	26	Universal permanent availability	Z	The percentage of marriages involving members of a particular group that includes a partner who is not in that group.
	27	Unmarried couple household	AA	The phenomenon that persons marry others like themselves more often than would be expected by chance.
	28	Victorianism	AB	Two adults, not related and of opposite sex, but no additional adults, and any children present are under 15 years old.

Short Essay

1. Using Sprecher and Mett's five basic elements of romantic ideals, select one popular TV show, movie, song, or other multimedia example and discuss how this contributes to or refutes contemporary patterns of mate selection.
2. Using the textbook's discussion of propinquity, analyze how Internet dating relationships refute this concept.

Critical Thinking

1. Compare the marriage rituals that you are most familiar with (what you would consider your "culture") to a culture you are less familiar with or that you would consider to be different from you. You may find some useful resources at "Marriage: Why is it a cross-cultural universal?" (http://anthropology.about.com/library/weekly/ aa070300a.htm?once+true&) or "Annotated Bibliography for Couples and Families Who Are Learning to Deal with Differences" (http://www.westernjustice.org/biblio.htm), but feel free to find other resources as well.
2. Explore the advertisements for "mail order brides" available on the Internet. What characteristics seem more "saleable"? Do you find repeated themes at different sites? If you were "shopping" for a mail-order partner, what characteristics would appeal to you? Consider writing your own advertisement either for yourself or for a future partner. Places to start include "The Mail Order Bride Guide" (http://www.planet-love.com/) or "Mail Order Brides" (www.latin-mail-order-brides.com/).

Additional Small Group Discussions

Your group has just started an Internet matchmaking service. Customers will pay a small fee to sign up and a larger fee if they get married. In addition, they will continue to pay a small annual fee for each year their marriage lasts.

You must design the questionnaire that customers will initially fill out. That, then, would be used by your service to arrange meetings for likely successful couples. What questions will you ask? Develop an extensive questionnaire that will gather the information you think will help you make good matches. What will you look for in matching couples? Will questions about race and looks be asked, and if so, would this be racism or "lookism"?

Will same sex couples be served by your business? If so, how would "marriage" be determined for purposes of your fees?

Answer Keys

Multiple Choice

1.	a	7.	d	13.	c	19.	b
2.	b	8.	c	14.	b	20.	b
3.	b	9.	c	15.	b	21.	d
4.	c	10.	c	16.	a	22.	b
5.	b	11.	a	17.	c	23.	a
6.	d	12.	b	18.	a		

True/False

1.	f		6.	f
2.	t		7.	t
3.	f		8.	t
4.	f		9.	t
5.	t		10.	f

Matching

1.	O	8.	S	15.	R	22.	X
2.	AA	9.	T	16.	N	23.	E
3.	J	10.	L	17.	B	24.	D
4.	C	11.	M	18.	Z	25.	H
5.	Q	12.	I	19.	K	26.	F
6.	P	13.	U	20.	Y	27.	AB
7.	W	14.	A	21.	V	28.	G

Short Essay

1. Using Sprecher and Mett's five basic elements of romantic ideals, select one popular TV show, movie, song, or other multimedia example and discuss how this contributes to ore refutes contemporary patterns of mate selection.
   a. Love at first sight
   b. Only one "true love" for each person

      c.   Love conquers all
      d.   True love is absolutely perfect
      e.   Choose partner for "love" rather than for other reasons

2.   Using the textbook's discussion of propinquity, analyze how Internet dating relationships refute this concept.
      a.   Most research is dated and may not reflect current trends
      b.   Many people have become more mobile and are willing to move to be with their partners
      c.   There are increases in the number of interracial relationships
      d.   Social class differences may not be as evident in cyberspace environments, although some people might argue that a certain amount of money is necessary to own or have access to computer equipment
      e.   On the other hand, most dating services provide an option for selecting dates from within a certain distance

Chapter 10 Varieties of Sexual Scripts

Learning Objectives

After reading this chapter, you should be able to
1. Discuss scripting theory in terms of who, what, where, when, and why with respect to sexual scripts.
2. Describe the multilayered nature of societal versus individual sexual scripting.
3. Outline control-repression models of sexuality and contrast them with full expression scripts.
4. Explain how couples go through each phase of scripting arriving at their own mutual sexual script.
5. Have an awareness of HIV/AIDS risk factors and protection methods.
6. Discuss rape in the context of sexual scripting and measurement difficulties.
7. Contrast biologically based scripts with social learning theory.

Chapter Outline

Thinking Ahead: If you could personally design today's sexual folkways, mores, and formal norms, what would they be like? Would premarital sex be acceptable? Would extramartial sex be approved? In what ways would your norms be the same as the ones currently in place? How would they be different? Why?

1) Sociological Theories of Human Sexuality
   a) Functionalism
   b) Conflict theory
   c) Symbolic interactionism/sexual scripts

2) Societal Scripts
   a) Control-repression scripts
      i) The traditional Christian control-repression script
      ii) Secular control-repression approaches
      iii) Inis Beag
   b) Full-expression scripts
      i) Mangaia
   c) Intermediate scripts
   d) Contemporary American values

3) Sex in a Time of AIDS

4) Gender Differences in Sexual Scripts
   a) The double standard
   b) Defining consent and rape

5) Learning Individual Scripts
    a)   Premarital sexuality
    b)   Initial sexual scenes
        i)   Adolescent options
        ii) Context of first intercourse
        iii) Reactions to first intercourse
        iv) Impact of premarital sex on marital relationships

6) Homosexual Scripts
    a)   Social construction of homosexuality
    b)   How many gays and lesbians?
    c)   The "why" of homosexuality
    d)   Homosexual "whats"

7) Constructing Marital Scripts
    a)   The "who" of marital sex
    b)   The "when" of marital sex
    c)   The "what" of marital sex

Rethinking in Context: Consider the sexual norms you proposed before reading the chapter. Do they still seem appropriate? How closely do they match your personal script? Where did you learn that? Do the norms you propose fit the economic and political realities of postindustrial America? Which norms would you like to see become laws, and which enforced informally? Why?

Multiple Choice Questions

1.   A functional analysis of sexuality supports the notion that
       a.   All societies have normative limits regarding sexual behavior
       b.   Premarital sex is permissible because it is a natural force and can contribute to procreation
       c.   The sex drive is not directly related to biology, and humans have choices about behavior
       d.   None of the above

2.   A key concept regarding sexuality for conflict theorists and feminists is
       a.   The double standard
       b.   Power
       c.   Natural sex drive
       d.   Social learning theory

3.   Which of the following is not one of the four levels of societal scripts mentioned in Chapter 10?
      a.   Personal scripts
      b.   Scenes
      c.   Mutual scripts
      d.   Ethnocentric scripts

4.   The most important element of sexual scripts is the
      a.   Who
      b.   Where
      c.   Why
      d.   When

5.   According to scripting theory, the idea that human beings have a natural, innate sex drive is
      a.   Strongly supported
      b.   Socially constructed
      c.   Not part of the construction of societal scripts
      d.   None of the above

6.   The primary "why" in the traditional Christian control-repression model
      a.   Pleasure
      b.   Nature
      c.   Procreation
      d.   Power

7.   In the full expression model, social and personal harm comes from _____ of the sex drive.
      a.   Expression
      b.   Repression
      c.   Exploration
      d.   None of the above

8.   The General Social Surveys reported that most Americans believe
      a.   Extramarital sex to be more objectionable then premarital sex
      b.   Premarital sex is always morally wrong
      c.   There is no change in attitudes about homosexuality
      d.   None of the above

9.   Increased incidence of HIV/AIDS has
     a.   Motivated some people to change their sexual practices and behaviors
     b.   Contributed to fear and stigma of groups such as gay men
     c.   Created crises of epidemic proportions in several African countries
     d.   All of the above

10. Husband exclusion laws provide an example of
     a.   Specific consent issues around rape
     b.   General consent issues around rape
     c.   Sociobiological theory
     d.   None of the above

11. One of the problems for prosecuting "date rape" includes
     a.   Mixed communication signals
     b.   Issues of consent
     c.   Lack of witnesses
     d.   All of the above

12. Who is most likely to have sex at the youngest age?
     a.   Black female
     b.   White male
     c.   Hispanic male
     d.   Hispanic female

13. The parental factor which seems to make the most difference in terms of teenage sexual
     activity is
     a.   Good communication
     b.   Presence in the home (intact family)
     c.   Permissiveness
     d.   None of the above

14. In terms of peer pressure and adolescent sexual activity, which of the following is most
     true?
     a.   Adolescents who use drugs and alcohol are less likely to have sex.
     b.   Adolescents who use drugs and alcohol are more likely to have sex.
     c.   Adolescents who have large circles of friends are more likely to have sex.
     d.   Adolescents who have lived in one place their whole life are more likely to have
          sex.

15.	The theory of relative consequences supports the idea that
	a.	Swedish women would have more positive attitudes about first sexual experiences because their society is more permissive than that in the United States
	b.	U.S. women would have positive attitudes about first sexual experiences if they were with a considerate partner
	c.	U.S. women would base their attitudes about first sexual experience on whether or not they felt pleasure
	d.	All of the above

16.	Kinsey was one of the first researchers to suggest
	a.	Sexual behavior can be measured on a continuum and is fluid or changing with time
	b.	There is no such thing as an exclusive heterosexual or exclusive homosexual
	c.	Over 30% of the population is gay or lesbian
	d.	None of the above

17.	"Coming out" is a process of disclosure associated with the _____ of homosexuality.
	a.	"why"
	b.	Discrimination
	c.	"where"
	d.	"when"

18.	Thompson concluded that the best predictor for extramarital affairs was
	a.	Age at marriage
	b.	Premarital sexual permissiveness
	c.	Length of marriage
	d.	All of the above are good predictors

19.	Couples who engage in a large amount of sexual activity during their first year of marriage or partnership are likely to
	a.	Have less sex later in the relationship
	b.	Remain more sexually active later in the relationship
	c.	Get divorced
	d.	Engage in comarital sex

20.	Sexual pleasure for women tends to
	a.	Be greater after the fifteenth year of marriage
	b.	Be less important than for men
	c.	Be greatest in adolescence
	d.	None of the above

True/False

1. The symbolic interactionist/scripting perspective would say that as humans we learn to be sexual.
2. The idea that couples should have sex at night and only in the bedroom is part of the "where" and "when" scripting aspects of sexuality.
3. Fear of excessive masturbation was part of the "full expression" script.
4. Mangaia is an isolated community in Ireland that practices the control-repression model of sexuality.
5. Over 80% of the U.S. population reports that they think homosexual activity is wrong, according to recent general social surveys.
6. Condom use reduces the odds of contracting sexually transmitted diseases but does not totally eliminate transmission.
7. Fantasy is more common during masturbation for moth men and women than during partnered sex.
8. There are several states in which a woman can be charged with raping a man.
9. Most rapes are committed by strangers.
10. Sexually active teenagers who had a sex education course know more about contraception and use it, as compared with those not exposed to such a program.

Matching

The terms introduced in this chapter are listed here in alphabetical order. Match the terms with the appropriate definition.

____	1	Acquaintance rape	A	A strong negative reaction to homosexuals and homosexuality.
____	2	Advocacy research	B	Having intercourse, even if consensual, with a person not considered old enough to give consent. In some states, only female victims are considered; others are gender-neutral.
____	3	AIDS	C	A man whose wife has extramarital coitus.
____	4	Bracketed scene	D	A social position that tends to override every other position a person holds.
____	5	Comarital sex	E	An interaction set apart from other day-to-day behavior by a definable beginning and end, during which particular roles and scripts apply.
____	6	Cuckold	F	Arrangement in which married partners allow each other to have extramarital sexual affairs and other freedoms not commonly associated with marriage.
____	7	Cunnilingus	G	Discrimination against homosexuals.
____	8	Date rape	H	Extramarital sex in which the married couple participates together.

_____	9 Erogenous zones	I	Fatal condition in which the body loses its natural ability to protect itself from disease.
_____	10 Extramarital sex	J	Intimate love for a person of the same sex.
_____	11 Fellatio	K	Nonconsensual intercourse imposed by a person known by the victim.
_____	12 Heterosexism	L	Nonconsensual sexual intercourse when the perpetrator and victim are voluntarily in a close relationship.
_____	13 HIV	M	Oral stimulation of the clitoris or vulva.
_____	14 Homophilia	N	Oral stimulation of the penis.
_____	15 Homophobia	O	Part of a rape law that makes it impossible to charge a husband with the rape of his wife.
_____	16 Husband exclusion clause	P	Parts of the body that, when stimulated, can lead to sexual arousal.
_____	17 Master status	Q	Sexual intercourse between a married person and someone not his or her spouse; adultery.
_____	18 Open marriage	R	Study done primarily to advance a political cause or point of view.
_____	19 Safe sex	S	The process of learning one's individual sexual script; sexual socialization.
_____	20 Sexualization	T	The virus that causes AIDS.
_____	21 Statutory rape	U	Use of condoms or other practices that significantly reduce the risk of spreading the AIDS-causing virus.

Short Essay

1. Your textbook author suggests that there are at least three manifestations of gender differences in terms of sexual scripts. Outline these differences and provide an example of each.
2. Brian has currently been interacting with a "female friend" he has met on the Internet. Tiffany, his wife of two years, knows he is spending a lot of time at the computer and suspects he may be having a "cyber" affair. Discuss where this activity would fall in terms of "scripting" activity by way of "what, when, why," and so on. Also provide advice for what you think Tiffany should do. Do you think your response would differ if you were the opposite gender? Why or why not? Support your response with factual information.

Critical Thinking

1. Read several of the articles available at the Centers for Disease Control site "HIV/AIDS Fact Sheets" (http://www.cdc.gov/him/pubs/facts.htm) on AIDS prevention and current

surveillance of the most-at-risk populations. Using this information design a program for your immediate community (i.e., dorm, town, church group, etc.) to help educate and prevent the spread of HIV/AIDS.

2. Investigate several online resources regarding rape such as "Marital Rape" (http://www.vaw.umn.edu/Vawnet/mrape.htm) or "Men Can Stop Rape" (http://www.mencanstoprape.org/) and discuss what you feel is or could be done in your community to help educate about or prevent rape. Also, discuss whether the web site is unbiased or advocacy-oriented.

3. Select one of the topics listed in the SIECUS report (http://www.siecus.org/pubs/srpt/ srpt0000.html) and discuss how the information you read about might be incorporated into a comprehensive sex education program for college-age students.

Additional Small Group Discussions

Consider the following scenario: A young man and woman go to a movie, and then return to her apartment, which is close to the theater. She has some joints, and they share one. They begin to make out, but before they get very far she says, "Stop–I'm really not ready for this." He stops, and they share another joint. They begin making out again, and this time shed most of their clothes before she says "Stop." He stops, and they have a beer. Then they start again, and this time she doesn't say no so they go all the way. The next morning, she feels like she was taken advantage of.

Was this rape? If so, what about the story would have to change to make it not be rape? If not, what change in the story would make it rape? Is there a difference between "moral rape" and "legal rape"? How would this woman probably answer a rape victim questionnaire if one of the questions was, "Did you ever have sex when the man got you drunk or stoned?"

Answer Keys

Multiple Choice

1.	a	6.	c	11.	d	16.	a
2.	b	7.	b	12.	c	17.	a
3.	d	8.	a	13.	b	18.	b
4.	c	9.	d	14.	b	19.	b
5.	b	10.	b	15.	a	20.	a

True/False

1.	t	6.	t
2.	t	7.	t
3.	f	8.	f
4.	f	9.	f
5.	f	10.	t

Matching

1.	K	8.	L	15.	A
2.	R	9.	P	16.	O
3.	I	10.	Q	17.	D
4.	E	11.	N	18.	F
5.	H	12.	G	19.	U
6.	C	13.	T	20.	S
7.	M	14.	J	21.	B

Short Essay

1. Your textbook author suggests that there are at least three manifestations of gender differences in terms of sexual scripts. Outline these differences and provide an example of each.
   a. Men separate sex from relationships
   b. Differences in images of body contact
   c. Differences in sexual fantasies

2. Brian has currently been interacting with a "female friend" he has met on the Internet. Tiffany, his wife of two years, knows he is spending a lot of time at the computer and suspects he may be having a "cyber" affair. Discuss where this activity would fall in terms of "scripting" activity by way of "what, when, why," and so on. Also provide advice for what you think Tiffany should do. Do you think your response would differ if you were the opposite gender? Why or why not? Support your response with factual information.
   a. Definitions of "sexual activity"
   b. Negotiating mutual scripts
   c. Differences in jealousy—emotional versus sexual infidelity

Chapter 11 Population and Family Planning

Learning Objectives

After reading this chapter, you should be able to
1. Briefly describe the importance of historical demographic trends.
2. Explain the concept of zero population growth and how this is important in terms of family planning.
3. Discuss the range of methods available for reducing the odds of pregnancy, including some of the current controversies around abstinence.
4. Describe some of the infertility treatments available and the accompanying legal, religious, moral, and ethical concerns.
5. Outline the possible avenues through which couples can adopt a child.
6. Articulate the ways in which macro-sociological trends interact with individual choices regarding family size.

Chapter Outline

Thinking Ahead: How many children would you like to have? Why? What social forces have affected this very personal decision of yours? Would adopting a child serve the same purposes for you as having a biological offspring? Why, why not? Is finding someone with similar views on these issues important in your mate-selection decisions?

1) Culture and Reproductive Regulation
    a) Latent fertility regulation
    b) Manifest fertility control
    c) Demographic transition theory
    d) Fertility choice in contemporary America

2) Fertility Reduction Methods
    a) Abstinence-based methods
    b) Coital methods
    c) Post-coital family planning
        i) The abortion issue
        ii) Having an abortion
        iii) Post-natal options

3) Childbirth and Fertility Enhancement
    a) Defining infertility
    b) Causes of infertility
    c) Assisted reproductive techniques
    d) Reproductive technology and culture lag
    e) Adoption

Rethinking in Context: Do you believe that there is an overpopulation problem in the world? If so, what should American foreign policy be with respect to the problem? How do personal, individual, and family decisions influence national and international demographic variables?

Multiple Choice Questions

1.   The potential number of births over a woman's lifetime is called _____ rate.
    a.   Fertility
    b.   Fecundity
    c.   Birth
    d.   None of the above

2.   Maria has an IUD. She could be classified as using which of the following forms of regulation?
    a.   Latent fertility
    b.   Manifest fertility
    c.   Interceptive fertility
    d.   None of the above

3.   Countries that are now highly developed saw the most rapid decline in death rates during which stage?
    a.   Secondary
    b.   Quaternary
    c.   Tertiary
    d.   Primary

4.   One theory for the decline of birth rate in the tertiary stage is
    a.   Children became an economic liability rather than a net labor benefit
    b.   There was an increase in infant mortality rate
    c.   People got married at an earlier age
    d.   All of the above

5.   During the 1900s, the highest birth rate was during the
    a.   1930s
    b.   1990s
    c.   1950s and 1960s
    d.   1920s

6.   Statistically speaking, which of the following women would be most likely "childfree" voluntarily?
     a.   Amy, who is White and has a master's degree
     b.   Mary, who is Hispanic and has an associate degree
     c.   Tamika, who is Black and has an associate degree
     d.   Eva, who is White and has a high school education

7.   The periodic abstinence method of contraception means couples
     a.   Avoid all sexual intercourse
     b.   Avoid sexual intercourse when the woman is menstruating
     c.   Avoid sexual intercourse when the woman is near ovulation
     d.   Have sexual intercourse at random times

8.   "The Pill," as a method of contraception,
     a.   Acts as a barrier method preventing sperm from reaching the egg
     b.   Tricks the body into thinking it is pregnant so ovulation does not occur
     c.   Aborts the fertilized egg
     d.   None of the above

9.   Which of the following is most true of vasectomies?
     a.   They make transmission of sperm through the vas deferens impossible
     b.   They are rarely reversible
     c.   They are very painful and risky surgical procedures
     d.   They make sex less pleasurable for men.

10. RU-486
     a.   Is illegal in the United States
     b.   Must be taken within seventy-two hours of intercourse
     c.   Is not very effective
     d.   All of the above

11. The Supreme Court case that was the precedent-setting case regarding abortions is called
     a.   State v. Roe
     b.   Doe v. Roe
     c.   Roe v. Wade
     d.   Griswald v. Oklahoma

12. Which of the following is most true regarding abortion?
     a.   Abortions are very risky medically speaking
     b.   Abortion rates in the United States are rising
     c.   White women are more likely to have abortions than women of color
     d.   Women in the 20–24 age group are least likely to have abortions

13.   Which of the following is most true regarding relinquishing a child?
        a.   More married women relinquish their infants than do unmarried women
        b.   Only about 2% of unmarried women relinquish their children
        c.   Relinquishment rates have increased since the 1970s
        d.   Poor women are more likely to relinquish their children

14.   Licensed physicians took over child delivering duties during
        a.   The Middle Ages
        b.   Colonial America
        c.   The mid-twentieth century
        d.   None of the above

15.   Which of the following is true regarding infertility?
        a.   Approximately 10% of American couples are infertile
        b.   Approximately 10% of American couples are "under-fertile"
        c.   Infertility is not the same thing as sterility
        d.   All of the above

16.   In vitro fertilization would most likely be used if the
        a.   Male partner has a low sperm count
        b.   Woman has blocked Fallopian tubes
        c.   Woman has a history of miscarriages
        d.   None of the above

17.   Artificial insemination would most likely be used if the
        a.   Male partner has a low sperm count
        b.   Woman is not ovulating regularly
        c.   Woman has blocked Fallopian tubes
        d.   All of the above

18.   A surrogate mother would most likely be used if the
        a.   Male partner has a low sperm count
        b.   Woman has endometriosis and a history of miscarriages
        c.   Woman has blocked Fallopian tubes
        d.   All of the above

19.   Which of the following is most true regarding adoption?
        a.   There are no unwanted, accidentally adopted children
        b.   Relinquishments are ahead of the demand for adopted children
        c.   About 10% of married-couple households have adopted children
        d.   There are more White children available for adoption than children of color

20. According to the theory of demographic transition, the death rate began to fall rapidly during the _____ stage
    a. Primary
    b. Secondary
    c. Tertiary
    d. Quaternary

True/False

1. The fertility rate often has been the same as the fecundity rate historically speaking.
2. Coitus interruptus is a latent fertility regulation.
3. In agricultural societies, fear of the death rate surpassing the birth rate was a common reason for being pronatalist.
4. The doubling time for North America is well over 100 years.
5. Couples who are involuntarily childless often experience great marital stress.
6. General abstinence is always 100% effective as a means of contraception.
7. The most common barrier method of contraception is the diaphragm.
8. A tubal ligation is a technique used to unblock the Fallopian tubes so infertile women can have children.
9. Women of color are more likely to have abortions than White women.
10. Couvades are common in the United States today.

Matching

The terms introduced in this chapter are listed here in alphabetical order. Match the terms with the appropriate definition.

_____	1	Abortifacient	A	A giving up or surrender of something; to give up legal rights to a child.
_____	2	Abortion ratio	B	A substance or device that causes abortion.
_____	3	Abortion	C	Number of abortions for every 1,000 known pregnancies.
_____	4	Abstinence	D	Surgical removal of the uterus.
_____	5	Adoption	E	The practice in which the husband of a woman in labor takes to his bed as though he were bearing the child.
_____	6	Artificial insemination	F	"Tying the tubes"; surgically cutting and tying the Fallopian tubes to prevent the passage of an ovum from the ovary to the uterus.
_____	7	Coitus interruptus	G	A biological potential of lifetime childbearing.
_____	8	Contraception	H	A person, usually a woman, who provides specialized care during childbirth.
_____	9	Couvade	I	A surgical procedure designed to make the transmission of sperm through the *vas deferens* impossible.

_____	10	Culture lag	J	A time discrepancy between technological change and change in nonmaterial aspects of culture such as laws and values.
_____	11	Doubling time	K	A woman who is paid for the use of her uterus to produce a baby.
_____	12	Fecundity	L	Actual number of births to a woman.
_____	13	Fertility	M	An agent that kills sperm, especially as a contraceptive.
_____	14	General abstinence	N	An object inserted into the uterus for the purpose of preventing pregnancy.
_____	15	Hysterectomy	O	Cultural practices that affect fertility without conscious intent by individuals.
_____	16	In vitro fertilization	P	Inability to achieve pregnancy or to carry a fetus to live birth.
_____	17	Infertility	Q	Intentional prevention of impregnation.
_____	18	Intrauterine device (IUD)	R	Joining of sperm and egg outside the body.
_____	19	Latent fertility regulation	S	Placing semen in the vagina or uterus by means other than sexual intercourse.
_____	20	Manifest fertility regulation	T	Practices used by persons with the conscious intent of affecting fertility.
_____	21	Midwife	U	Surgical removal of the ovaries.
_____	22	Ovariectomy	V	Taking into one's own family and raising as one's own child.
_____	23	Periodic abstinence	W	Termination of a pregnancy before the fetus can survive outside the uterus.
_____	24	Relinquishment	X	The number of years it would take a particular population to double in size if it continued to grow at a given rate.
_____	25	Spermicide	Y	The practice of attempting to avoid conception by refraining from intercourse at certain times of the menstrual cycle.
_____	26	Surrogate mother	Z	The practice of attempting to prevent conception in which the penis is withdrawn from the vagina before ejaculation.
_____	27	Tubal ligation	AA	The practice of completely avoiding sexual intercourse.
_____	28	Vasectomy	AB	The practice of refraining from indulging some appetite such as food, drink, or a particular sexual practice.

Short Essay

1. Discuss how the demographic transition theory explains changes in birth rates.

2. Describe why general abstinence might not be 100% effective as a means of contraception.
3. Discuss the difficulties with defining "infertility."

Critical Thinking

1. Do you think the United States and other advanced nations have a responsibility to help people in countries that are still going through a population explosion? Explain. If the U.S. does have a responsibility, what, according to the Theory of Demographic Transition, would be the most effective things that could be done?
2. Your textbook author suggests that many young people know more about the proper use of birth control and/or how to get an abortion than they do about relinquishing parental rights. Your task is to design a brochure to help educate young people on this issue.
3. Locate more information on the cultural practice of the couvade. Why do you think this is not more routinely practiced in the United States? You might also locate other customs or tradition surrounding pregnancy and childbirth that are practiced in cultures outside the United States.

Additional Small Group Discussions

Would you say your parents' parenting styles were permissive, authoritarian, authoritative, or some combination? What would you like your parenting style to be? Work as a group to produce a small brochure that would explain good parenting styles to a high-school level family relations class. Make sure the brochure is based on good research and theory.

Answer Keys

Multiple Choice

1.	b	6.	a	11.	c	16.	b
2.	b	7.	c	12.	c	17.	a
3.	a	8.	b	13.	b	18.	b
4.	a	9.	a	14.	c	19.	a
5.	c	10.	b	15.	d	20.	b

True/False

1.	f	6.	f
2.	f	7.	f
3.	t	8.	f
4.	t	9.	f
5.	t	10.	f

Matching

1.	B	8.	Q	15.	D	22.	U
2.	C	9.	E	16.	R	23.	Y
3.	W	10.	J	17.	P	24.	A
4.	AB	11.	X	18.	N	25.	M
5.	V	12.	G	19.	O	26.	K
6.	S	13.	L	20.	T	27.	F
7.	Z	14.	AA	21.	H	28.	I

Short Essay

1. Discuss how the demographic transition theory explains changes in birth rates.
   a. Industrialized nations are able to increase production to keep up with population growth.
   b. In agricultural societies, fear of death rate exceeding birth rate encouraged prenatal attitudes.
   c. Increasing productivity produced better nutrition and more sanitary living conditions.

2. Describe why general abstinence might not be 100% effective as a means of contraception.
   a. Failure rates are calculated as the percent of women who get pregnant in a year while using the method.
   b. Rape or incest can result in pregnancy.
   c. People might plan to practice abstinence but get "carried away."

3. Discuss the difficulties with defining "infertility."
   a. Issues of measurement—may be including biological factors as well as voluntary procedures such as hysterectomy or vasectomy.
   b. Average rates for conception vary by age.
   c. "Under-fertility" may be different from infertility.

Chapter 12 Negotiating Marriages

Learning Objectives

After reading this chapter, you should be able to
1. Explain changing role structures and relationships.
2. Understand conjugal power in terms of resource theory and gender.
3. Describe how newlywed role decisions may differ from people who are married for longer periods of time.
4. Discuss the various roles couples might negotiate, including but not limited to provided, housekeeper, sexual, recreation, religious, and kinship.
5. Explain the research difficulties with concepts like "happiness."
6. Outline some of the key issues related to marital satisfaction.
7. Discuss developmental theories, particularly in terms of marital satisfaction and the "empty nest" period.
8. Describe how marital quality might change over the course of a lifetime.

Chapter Outline

Thinking Ahead: How much independence do you think husbands and wives should have from each other? Which partner, if either, should have the final say in such matters as how to raise children, purchasing new furniture, or where to live? If you think they should have equal say, how will the matter get resolved when they disagree? Says who? How can you measure whether a marriage is good or bad?

1) Changing Meanings of Marriage

2) Conjugal Power
    a)   Family power and early sociology
    b)   Resource theory
    c)   Gender-based conceptions of power
    d)   Human capital and empowerment theories

3) Marital Roles and Scripts
    a)   Couple role relationships
        i)   A role typology
            (1) Housekeeper
            (2) Provider
            (3) Sexual
            (4) Kinship
            (5) Recreational
            (6) Therapeutic
            (7) Child-care

           (8) Child-socialization
           (9) Religion
      ii) The provider and kinship roles
      iii) The recreation role
           (1) Individual activities
           (2) Joint activities
           (3) Parallel activities
      iv) The therapeutic role
  b) Constructing postindustrial marital scripts
  c) Generalized mutual scripts

4) Marital Quality
  a) Measuring marital quality
  b) Correlates of quality: Identifying marital strengths
      i) Socioeconomic status
      ii) Race
      iii) Religion
      iv) Class, age, and racial homogamy
      v) Work/family arrangements
      vi) Presence of children
      vii) Communication, support, and sexuality
      viii) Maintenance behaviors

5) Marriage in the Middle and Later Years
  a) Life cycle of a marriage
  b) Marital satisfaction and the life cycle
  c) Post-parental couples
  d) Post-launch transitions
  e) Post-retirement couples
  f) Death, grief, and mourning

Rethinking in Context: If you could ask a couple five questions to find out how good their marriage is, what would those questions be? Why? Would your questions be different for young than for old couples? Why, why not? Assuming you get married, what you would like to be able to say about your marriage when you look back at it at age eighty-five?

Multiple Choice Questions

1. John and Josephine were recently married and have not had to discuss "who will do
    what" in terms of their relationship. They live in a culture with prescribed duties for men
    and women. Their relationship would be an example of
    a. Androgyny
    b. Post-industrial negotiation
    c. Spontaneous consensus
    d. Normative marital disjunctions

2. Joe has said that he will take away the car keys from Susan if she does not have his
    dinner ready on time. They only have one vehicle and Susan relies on it to go to her job.
    Joe would be using which type of power?
    a. Negotiated
    b. Legitimate
    c. Illegitimate
    d. Influence

3. The "norm of reciprocity" is associated with which theory?
    a. Weber's theory of conjugal power
    b. Social exchange or resource theory
    c. Developmental theory
    d. Sociobiological theory

4. Brinkerhoff and Lupri studied socioeconomic status and decision-making processes
    between couples. They found that
    a. As education, occupation, and income of couples increased, they made more
        joint decisions
    b. As education, occupation, and income of couples increased, they made more
        independent but equal decisions
    c. "Pooling" resources is more likely to happen with increased income
    d. None of the above

5. The human capital analysis of marriage uses which of the following?
    a. Functionalism
    b. Resource theory
    c. Both (a) and (b) above
    d. Sociobiology

6. The empowerment model operates on which of the following principles?
    a. One person wins and the other loses
    b. Both people can use resources to increase the resources of the other partner
    c. Neither partner has any power and both are frustrated
    d. All of the above

7. Which role focuses on supplying the money and material goods necessary to support the family?
    a. Housekeeper
    b. Kinship
    c. Child-socialization
    d. Provider

8. Which role involves the responsibility of instilling the values, attitudes, skills, and behaviors required by children for success in society?
    a. Recreational
    b. Therapeutic
    c. Child-socialization
    d. Kinship

9. Greg and Ginny have a joint checking account. They put all their money into it and each has access to it. Which distribution system are they using?
    a. Housekeeping allowance system
    b. Independent management system
    c. Pooling system
    d. Whole wage system

10. A "vital" marriage is likely to have
    a. little recreational time together
    b. many joint activities
    c. a weak therapeutic role foundation
    d. all of the above

11. Marital stability is one of the key concepts in determining marital satisfaction. Some researchers have found
    a. Low levels of marital stability usually mean high marital satisfaction
    b. Marriages can be stable yet unsatisfying and that fact seems related to how much opportunity is available for alternative spouses
    c. There is less marital stability when couples move frequently
    d. None of the above

12.   Which is most true regarding marital satisfaction?
    a.   Economic hardship tends to lower marital satisfaction
    b.   Education tends to increase happiness especially for women
    c.   Couples who attend religious services have higher levels of satisfaction
    d.   All of the above are true

13.   Regarding traditional attitudes, which is most true?
    a.   When women develop less traditional attitudes, they report quality of marriage as going up
    b.   When women develop less traditional attitudes, they report quality of marriage as going down
    c.   When men develop less traditional attitudes, they report quality of marriage as staying the same
    d.   All of the above

14.   Generally speaking, voluntarily childless women report
    a.   Lower levels of marital satisfaction
    b.   High levels of marital cohesion
    c.   Mixed levels of marital satisfaction
    d.   None of the above

15.   Which of the following has been associated with high marital satisfaction?
    a.   Higher rates of self-disclosure
    b.   Expressions of love, support, and affection
    c.   Laughter and positive nonverbal communication
    d.   All of the above

16.   Which of the following is not one of the five common types of relationship maintenance behaviors?
    a.   Positivity
    b.   Openness
    c.   Assurances
    d.   Fighting fairly

17.   The "U-shaped" curve of marital satisfaction
    a.   Means there is a gradual decline in satisfaction over the life span
    b.   Means that satisfaction tends to start high, lessen during raising of children, then finishes high in later life
    c.   Has mixed research support
    d.   Both (b) and (c) above

18.   At which stage would men be most likely to suffer a "mid-life crisis"?
      a.   Post-launch
      b.   Post-retirement
      c.   Post-partum
      d.   Post-operative

19.   Which is most true for older Americans?
      a.   Social security provides adequate income for most people
      b.   Over 10% live in poverty
      c.   There is no difference by ethnicity in poverty levels
      d.   None of the above

20.   Who is at most risk for suicide after the death of a spouse?
      a.   Older woman
      b.   Older man
      c.   Younger woman
      d.   Younger man

True/False

1.   Women who have more resources tend to have more power in their relationships.
2.   The "care perspective" focuses on autonomy, self-interest, rational thoughts, and abstract standards of rights and justice.
3.   The female whole wage system gives wives sole responsibility for household finances.
4.   Intrinsic marriages are primarily for convenience.
5.   A couple in a conflict-habituated marriage will often fight in public.
6.   Unemployed people tend to report high levels of marital satisfaction.
7.   Couples with large age discrepancies report low levels of marital satisfaction.
8.   Several research studies report little difference between happiness levels of women who worked inside or outside the home.
9.   Couples with very young children rarely get divorced.
10. Satisfaction with sexual communication is unrelated to overall marital satisfaction.

Matching

The terms introduced in this chapter are listed here in alphabetical order. Match the terms with the appropriate definition.

_____	1 Adjustment	A	A man whose wife has died.
_____	2 Ageism	B	The ability to shape the thinking and behavior of a decision maker.
_____	3 Authority	C	A woman whose husband has died.
_____	4 Bereavement	D	Actions taken by participants to preserve ongoing relationships.

_____	5	Conjugal power	E	Agreement arrived at without consideration by the parties involved, based on commonly held assumptions that are often derived from tradition.

_____ 5 Conjugal power

E Agreement arrived at without consideration by the parties involved, based on commonly held assumptions that are often derived from tradition.

_____ 6 Developmental tasks

F Agreement between actors about how a role should be played.

_____ 7 Empty nest syndrome

G Characterized by good luck, pleasure, satisfaction, or joy.

_____ 8 Grief

H Deep mental and emotional anguish.

_____ 9 Happy

I Discrimination or prejudice based on age, especially against the elderly.

_____ 10 Illegitimate power

J Fulfillment of a desire, need, or appetite; contentment derived from having needs met.

_____ 11 Influence

K Marriages with a "why" other than intimate expression; a marriage of convenience for economic or other reasons.

_____ 12 Intrinsic marriages

L Marriages with the "why" of maintaining the intimacy of the relationship between husband and wife.

_____ 13 Mourning

M Power exercised in socially approved ways; legitimate power.

_____ 14 Postparental period

N Power exercised without the consent of the governed, or in socially unapproved ways, usually by coercion.

_____ 15 Power

O Resistant to change, self-restoring, consistently dependable.

_____ 16 Relationship maintenance behaviors

P Role loss after a child has left the home resulting in depression, identity crisis, and lowered well-being.

_____ 17 Retirement

Q The ability of spouses to affect each other's behavior.

_____ 18 Role consensus

R The act or means of adapting, corresponding, or conforming.

_____ 19 Satisfaction

S The condition of being deprived of a loved one by death.

_____ 20 Spontaneous consensus

T The probability that one actor within a social relationship will be in a position to carry out his or her own will (despite resistance).

_____ 21 Stable

U The socially constructed expectations regarding reactions to death.

_____ 22 Utilitarian marriages

V Time in the family life cycle after the children leave home as adults.

_____ 23 Widow

W To withdraw from one's paid occupation.

_____ 24 Widower

X Undertakings or objectives associated with a particular stage in the life of an individual or life cycle of a family.

Short Essay

1. Phillip and Andrea have been best friends since high school. They enjoy many of the same kinds of activities, like going out with other people, and enjoy home remodeling together. Classify their relationship using Cuber and Haroff's typology and discuss how people might move or change categories.
2. Discuss Duval's framework for life cycles. How or why is it useful (or not) for many couples today?

Critical Thinking

1. "Boomerang" children or "crowded empty nests" are becoming more commonplace today as adult children return home to live with their parents. Discuss what tensions, conflicts, and issues are likely to arise when this situation occurs and what you think could be done to help alleviate them.
2. Discuss the Social Security debate. Do you have any personal concerns about whether there will be enough money there for you upon retirement (if you are retired, whether it will last long enough)? What are some of the possible plans being discussed by politicians today? Research your response using Internet or other sources to create an informal argument. The AARP site (http://www.aarp.org/socialsecurity/) is a good place to begin.
3. Consider the major correlates of power. Do you think each of these is a cause of happiness or the result of other combinations of variables?

Additional Small Group Discussions

1. Revisit the discussion you had from Chapter 9 regarding the questionnaire you constructed for the mate-matching service. Are there questions you might want to add based on information from this chapter about happy and stable marriages?

2. Consider Pahl's five major distributive systems:

        a. The female whole wage system
        b. The male whole wage system
        c. The housekeeping allowance system
        d. The independent management system
        e. The pooling system

What system did your parents, or the couple you knew best as a child, use? What are the advantages and disadvantages of that system? What would you like to use if you get married? How would you handle it if your spouse wanted to use a different system?

Answer Keys

Multiple Choice

1.	c	6.	b	11.	b	16.	d
2.	c	7.	d	12.	d	17.	d
3.	b	8.	c	13.	b	18.	a
4.	b	9.	c	14.	b	19.	b
5.	c	10.	b	15.	d	20.	b

True/False

1.	t	6.	f
2.	f	7.	f
3.	t	8.	t
4.	f	9.	t
5.	f	10.	f

Matching

1.	R	7.	P	13.	U	19.	J
2.	I	8.	H	14.	V	20.	E
3.	M	9.	G	15.	T	21.	O
4.	S	10.	N	16.	C	22.	K
5.	Q	11.	B	17.	W	23.	C
6.	X	12.	L	18.	F	24.	A

Short Essay

1. Phillip and Andrea have been best friends since high school. They enjoy many of the same kinds of activities, like going out with other people, and enjoy home remodeling together. Classify their relationship using Cuber and Haroff's typology and discuss how people might move or change categories.
    a. This is a passive-congenial marriage under the utilitarian category; it might become devitalized if they did not share similar interests and might become more vital if they built a stronger emotional connection.

2. Discuss Duval's framework for life cycles. How or why is it useful (or not) for many couples today?
    a. Does not address childfree couples
    b. Does not address divorce and remarriage
    c. Empty nest may be rare
    d. Does not account for family formation

Chapter 13 Parents and Children

Learning Objectives

After reading this chapter, you should be able to
1. Contrast the socialization processes between more traditional societies and more contemporary societies.
2. Discuss some of the characteristics of preindustrial socialization practices.
3. Explain how many couples' scripts change after becoming parents.
4. Outline some of the concerns with nonparental child care.
5. Briefly describe the major theorists' ideas about socialization and childrearing.
6. Discuss the controversy over the role of punishment in childrearing.
7. Explain whether or not the mother's work patterns have any influence over child development.
8. Comment on issues relevant to single-parent households and gay and lesbian parent households.

Chapter Outline

Thinking Ahead: What things about the way you were raised would you like to change if you raise (or have raised) children? What things would you like to do the same way? What things have changed about society since your parents were young that call for different ways of raising children today?

1) Socialization in Context
   a) Socialization continuum
   b) Historical images of parents and children
   c) Emergence of modern childhood

2) Becoming Parents: Rescripting the Conjugal Unit
   a) Reasons for having children
   b) Expenses of having children
   c) Transition to parenthood
   d) Traditionalizing influence of parenthood
   e) Explanations for gender-divergent parenting

3) Nonparental Child Care
   a) Users of nonparental child care
   b) Consequences of nonparental child care

4) Theoretical Images of Socialization
   a) Psychological theories of socialization
      i) The psychoanalytic view: Freud

      ii)   Socialization as a lifelong process: Erikson
      iii) Cognitive development: Piaget

   b)   Sociological and social-psychological theories
      i)   Social control and bonding: Hirshi
         (1) Belief
         (2) Attachment
         (3) Commitment
         (4) Involvement
      ii)   Toward social learning: Skinner and Bandura
      iii) Symbolic interactionism
   c)   Genetics critique

5) Socialization in Practice
   a)   Discipline and punishment
   b)   Parenting scripts
      i)   Authoritarian
      ii)   Permissive
      iii) Authoritative

6) Multigenerational Grandparent Families with Children
   a)   Parents and adult children
   b)   Grandparenting
      i)   Companionate
      ii)   Remote
      iii) Involved

7) Single Parents and Children

8) Gay and Lesbian Parents and Children

Rethinking in Context: Have you changed any of your opinions about raising children as a result of reading this chapter? Do you think children should have all the same rights as adults? If not, which should they not have? Should parents be made legally responsible for the criminal acts of their children? If such laws were passed, how, from the various theoretical perspectives, would the socialization process be affected? If you ran an adoption agency, would you give preference in adoptions to married couples over single individuals or gay couples? Why or why not?

Multiple Choice Questions

1. Most socialization of children occurs in
    a. The extended family
    b. Primary relationships
    c. Secondary relationships
    d. Both (b) and (c)

2. At point C on the socialization continuum, where there is essentially no socialization, each generation
    a. Basically replicates the older generation
    b. Redefines itself
    c. Goes through a period of slow social change
    d. None of the above

3. Children without siblings have
    a. Considerably higher educational and intellectual achievement than do children with siblings
    b. No more health problems than children with siblings
    c. No more adjustment problems than children with siblings
    d. All of the above

4. Concerning pronatalism, which of the following statements is most true?
    a. Catholics prefer more children than Protestants
    b. Whites prefer more children than Blacks
    c. Hispanics prefer fewer children than any other group
    d. People from large families want fewer children

5. Current research suggests that the birth of the first child can lead to
    a. Increased marital satisfaction
    b. Declining marital satisfaction
    c. Women enjoying their jobs more
    d. No change in marital quality

6. Which of the following is not one of the characteristics of the transition to parenthood, according to Alice Rossi?
    a. Parenthood is irrevocable
    b. Parenthood can be abrupt
    c. Parenthood affects couple relationships
    d. Parenthood is not supported by cultural norms

7.   The traditionalizing influence of parenthood
      a.   Means both parents are likely to spend the same amount of time in child-care activities
      b.   Means women assume more responsibility for child care and men increase their responsibility for working outside the home
      c.   Is related to the "sex-irreducible role" of parenthood
      d.   Both (b) and (c)

8.   The research concerning parental closeness suggests that children are best off when
      a.   The mother takes most of the responsibility for childrearing
      b.   There is a sense of closeness with both parents
      c.   The child get used to several different child-care persons
      d.   None of the above

9.   Which group is least likely to use nonparental child care?
      a.   Whites
      b.   Blacks
      c.   Hispanics
      d.   Asians

10.   From the meta-analysis conducted by Russell, which compared children whose mothers were their care providers with children who spent at least some time in nonmaternal care, which of the following conclusions is correct?
      a.   Little difference was discovered
      b.   Nonwhite children fared better than White children
      c.   Boys fared more poorly in nonmaternal care than girls
      d.   All of the above

11.   The ideas regarding child socialization, that most adult problems can be blamed on things that went wrong very early in the child's life, can be attributed primarily to
      a.   Erikson
      b.   Piaget
      c.   Skinner
      d.   Freud

12.   The theorist who used juvenile delinquency as a measurement for socialization practices was
      a.   Piaget
      b.   Freud
      c.   Hirshi
      d.   Cooley

13.   Karen rewards Justin with a colored sticker every time he cleans up his own toys. Karen is using a system of rewards most consistent with which theorist?
       a.   Skinner
       b.   Piaget
       c.   Freud
       d.   Mead

14.   The idea that children go through three stages, preparatory, play, and game, is attributed to Mead and is associated with which theory of socialization?
       a.   Psychodynamic
       b.   Behavioral
       c.   Social learning
       d.   Symbolic interactionism

15.   Matthew believes that children should respect their parents and often will punish Robin, his three-year-old daughter, for not obeying him. His style of parenting could be classified as
       a.   Permissive
       b.   Authoritative
       c.   Authoritarian
       d.   Laissez faire

16.   Parenting styles are affected by
       a.   Race
       b.   The nature of the parent's work in the paid labor force
       c.   Class
       d.   All of the above

17.   Research suggests that the greatest factor determining the amount of personal assistance or caregiving an adult child provides for her/his parent is
       a.   Based on finances
       b.   Geographic distance
       c.   Level of education
       d.   Occupational prestige

18.   Nelda always sends her grandchildren money for their birthdays and for holidays. She lives several states away from them and cannot visit often because of her health. She could be classified as which type of grandparent?
       a.   Companionate
       b.   Involved
       c.   Remote
       d.   Disinterested

19.   Generalizing from the research reported concerning single-parent families, which of the
       following statements is most true?
       a.   Children in father-surrogate households are worse off than those in single-parent
             households
       b.   Children in single-parent households tend to do better in school
       c.   Socioeconomic status accounts for much of the difference reported between one-
             and two-parent households
       d.   None of the above

20.   Which of the following statements is most correct regarding lesbian mothers?
       a.   They are likely to sexually molest their children
       b.   They are good male role models for their sons
       c.   They are likely to be more child-oriented than some heterosexual mothers
       d.   They are more likely to be depressed than heterosexual mothers

True/False

1.   Generation gaps are common in orderly replacement societies.
2.   Early historians all agree on how the concept of childhood developed.
3.   Most parents today express no preferences concerning the gender of their children.
4.   If a couple have three children in their household, about 48% of their income will be spent
      on the children.
5.   Transition to parenthood is more difficult for middle-class families than for working-class
      ones.
6.   For single working mothers, fathers provide over 50% of the child care.
7.   According to Rowe, the genetic influence is the major contribution parents make in their
      children's lives.
8.   Spanking is illegal in Sweden.
9.   Reportedly, about 90% of parents in the United States spank their children.
10.   Caregiving for elderly parents affects most daughters negatively.

Matching

The terms introduced in this chapter are listed here in alphabetical order. Match the terms with the
appropriate definition.

_____	1	Contingency	A	A person who provides an image with which an observer identifies and may wish to emulate.
_____	2	Daughter track	B	Changes in behavior that result from watching others, without direct rewards or punishments to oneself.
_____	3	Discipline	C	Role expectation that a daughter will have primary responsibility for familial elder care, in addition to other tasks.

	4	Game stage	D	To Mead, the internalized image persons have of the expectations of society as a whole.
_____	5	Generalized other	E	To Mead, the third stage of observational development, beginning about age seven or eight, in which children actually assume roles in interaction with others.
_____	6	Imitation	F	A contingency that decreases the probability that a preceding behavior will recur.
_____	7	Libido	G	A contingency that increases the probability that a preceding behavior will recur.
_____	8	Looking-glass self	H	An individual's sense of identity.
_____	9	Maternal deprivation theory	I	Continuing interaction by individuals in more than one role; characterized by personal, direct, and intimate interaction.
_____	10	Modeling	J	Continuing interaction by individuals in only one role; characterized by impersonal interaction for a specific, practical purpose.
_____	11	Observational learning	K	Repetition of an observed set of behavior patterns.
_____	12	Orderly replacement	L	Socialization in which each generation is an essential duplicate of the preceding generation.
_____	13	Play stage	M	The repetition of an observed behavior.
_____	14	Preparatory stage	N	The tendency of couples to develop more traditional, gender-specific, roles once they have a child.
_____	15	Primary relationship	O	The theory, now largely discredited, that a child must have a warm, continuous, exclusive, and virtually full-time emotional involvement with its mother.
_____	16	Punishment	P	To Cooley, the concept that we come to see ourselves as we think other persons see us.
_____	17	Reward	Q	To Freud, the basic energy, primarily sexual in nature, that provides the driving force of all human behavior.
_____	18	Role model	R	To Mead, the developmental socialization process by which children learn from others.
_____	19	Secondary relationship	S	To Mead, the second stage of observational development, up to about age seven or eight, characterized by playing at being other persons.
_____	20	Self	T	To Mead, the time during which the infant lacks the capacity for extensive language use.

	21	Stages of observation	U	To Skinner, a change in the environment that affects the behavior preceding it.
	22	Traditionalizing influence of parenthood	V	To train by instruction and practice; especially to teach self-control.

Short Essay

1. Discuss the research comparing single-parent households with two-parent households. What are the main areas of difference or concern? What are some of the research dilemmas in generalizing conclusions?
2. Much of the popular press and some of the research on caregiving for elderly parents have focused on the "problems" or negative outcomes. What does the research suggest in terms of positive outcomes?

Critical Thinking

1. Watch a current movie that has examples of relationships between parents and children. Using Baumrinds' styles of parenting, discuss the characters in the movie in terms of parenting style. Be specific and concrete with your examples.
2. Imagine that you are a mental health professional who has a new couple client who is lesbian mothers. They are concerned about the social stigma their children might face when moving to a new community. Your task is to research some of these potential issues via the Internet or other resources and then provide a list of "pointers" or advice that you think might be helpful to them. Several good places to begin include (http://www.lesbian.org/lesbian-moms/articles.html) or (http://www.colage.org/) or (http://www.apa.org/pi/l&bbks.html).

Additional Small Group Discussions

On the next page, find a score sheet for prospective adoptions. Remember that this is a "rubric" for deciding what parents and children would be a good match. You are not interviewing the children or their prospective adopters at this point.

PRELIMINARY ADOPTION SCREENING SCORES

The Mycollege adoption agency has many more parents who want to adopt than it has available healthy infants. You are to develop an objective screening form that helps determine which parents will actually get a chance to adopt a child.

Determine the number of points that might be possible for each of the following categories and how the points might be distributed within that category. For number one, for example, you might decide that income doesn't matter, so no discriminations are made in that category. In effect, income is worth zero points. Or, you might decide that income should be worth as many as ten points. That might be distributed in any number of ways. Some possibilities are:

    a. Below poverty level=0 points; above poverty level=10 points.
    b. Below poverty level=0 points; poverty level to median family=5 points; above median
        family=10 points.
    c. One point for each $10,000 in income, up to 10 points.
    d. Below poverty level=5 points; poverty to 95th percentile, 10 points; above 95th
        percentile, 0 points.

    For ease of scoring, the number of overall points must total 100. Make sure that the instrument will make significant distinctions among potential adopting parents; it is not useful if everyone gets 95 points or above. Since there are 10 categories, you might begin with the assumption that each is worth 10 points, then increase and decrease values as desired. Keep in mind the best interests of the children.

1. Current income of adopting family   _____ pts.
        How determined?

2. Racial/ethnic parent-child compatibility   _____ pts.
        How determined?

3. Educational level of parent(s)   _____ pts.

4. Legal background of parent(s)   _____ pts.
        Consider arrests, conviction, misdemeanors, felonies, etc.

5. Relationship status of parents(s)   _____ pts.
        Consider whether couple is married, stability of relationship, whether applicant is a single
        person, whether it is a same or opposite-sex couple, etc.

6. Extended family possibilities   _____ pts.
        Consider whether the child will have siblings, close cousins, aunts and uncles,
        grandparents, other real or fictive kin.

7. Necessity for non-parental child care   _____ pts.
      Consider whether non-parental child care is likely to be used, etc.

8. Parental employment(s)   _____ pts.
      Steadiness of work history, one or both parents work, etc.

9. Child-rearing attitudes   _____ pts.
      Are parents knowledgeable about children, do they believe in spanking, etc.

10. Other criteria   _____ pts.

Answer Keys

Multiple Choice

1.	d	6.	d	11.	d	16.	d
2.	b	7.	d	12.	c	17.	b
3.	d	8.	b	13.	a	18.	c
4.	a	9.	c	14.	d	19.	c
5.	b	10.	c	15.	c	20.	c

True/False

1.	f	6.	f
2.	f	7.	t
3.	f	8.	t
4.	t	9.	t
5.	t	10.	f

Matching

1.	U	7.	Q	13.	S	19.	J
2.	C	8.	P	14.	T	20.	H
3.	V	9.	O	15.	I	21.	R
4.	E	10.	K	16.	F	22.	N
5.	D	11.	B	17.	G		
6.	M	12.	L	18.	A		

Short Essay

1. Discuss the research comparing single-parent households with two-parent households. What are the main areas of difference or concern? What are some of the research dilemmas in generalizing conclusions?
    a. Correlation between juvenile delinquency and single-parent households
    b. Economic/financial issues
    c. Gender differences
    d. Classroom behavior problems
    e. School success
    f. Ethnicity

2. Much of the popular press and some of the research on caregiving for elderly parents have focused on the "problems" or negative outcomes. What does the research suggest in terms of positive outcomes?
   a. Children feel appreciated
   b. Brings sense of gratification
   c. Can create more emotional closeness
   d. Parents provide advice to adult children
   e. Greater sense of reciprocity between parents and children

Chapter 14 Crisis and Violence in Families

Learning Objectives

After reading this chapter, you should be able to

1. Explain Hill's ABC-X and McCubbin's double ABC-X models for family stress and crisis.
2. Discuss how social construction and social movement theory helps us understand how ideas about what is right and wrong in families can change over time.
3. Briefly trace the history of child abuse as a social problem.
4. Discuss some of the research and measurement issues and problems with family violence as a variable.
5. Outline Walker's cycle of violence, and compare her perspective with that measured by the Conflict Tactics Scale.
6. Briefly trace the history of the shelter movement.
7. Discuss the differences between individual and family counseling approaches for treating family violence.
8. Describe potential future issues concerning family violence.

Chapter Outline

Thinking Ahead: What are the most serious problems in families today? If you had to measure the amount of family violence in America, how would you go about it? What is your definition of child abuse? In what ways should the government be involved in reducing family violence? How would your answers be likely to differ from those given by your parents when they were your age? Your grandparents?

1) Defining Family Crisis
   a)   Coping with stress
   b)   Hill's ABC-X model
       i)   The stressor event
       ii) Resources
       iii) Definition of the stressor
       iv) The crisis
   c)   McCubbin's double ABC-X model

2) The Social Construction of Child Abuse
   a)   Social movement theory
       i)   Incipiency
       ii) Coalescence
       iii) Institutionalization
       iv) Fragmentation
       v)   Demise

    b)   History of child abuse
    c)   Types and frequency of child abuse

3) Spouse Abuse
    a)   Spouse abuse prior to the post-industrial era
    b)   The shelter movement
    c)   Fragmentation of the battered women movement

4) Research on Family Violence
    a)   Correlates of family violence
    b)   Other forms of family violence
    c)   Alternative theoretical explanations of family violence

5) Other Family Troubles and Responses
    a)   Responses to spouse abuse
    b)   Alcohol abuse
    c)   Counseling
        i)   Individual
        ii) Family
    d)   Social change

Rethinking in Context: What family-related issues might become social problems in the future? What groups would be likely advocates for the issue? Should the legal authorities become more or less involved in family violence than is now the case? Why or why not should spanking be considered a form of child abuse? Would you turn your parents in if you thought they were abusing you?

Multiple Choice Questions

1.   The Smith family has decided to move to a new state for better job opportunities. According to Hill's ABC-X model, this would be which type of stressor?
        a.   Community
        b.   Internal
        c.   Crisis
        d.   Major

2.   Which of the following could be a resource according to Hill's ABC-X model?
        a.   Money
        b.   Religious faith
        c.   Good health
        d.   All of the above

3.   Which of the following concepts is associated with McCubbin's double ABC-X model of family stress?
      a.   Effect of time
      b.   Pileup
      c.   Adaptation
      d.   All of the above

4.   Which of the following is not one of Mauss's stages of social movement theory?
      a.   Incipiency
      b.   Demise
      c.   Convalescence
      d.   Fragmentation

5.   Historically speaking, most family members were dealt with by whom?
      a.   Neighbors
      b.   Pastors
      c.   Extended family members
      d.   All of the above

6.   The first formal definition of child abuse happened in
      a.   1912
      b.   The 1950s
      c.   1974
      d.   1995

7.   Which of the following is not a symptom of fragmentation of the child-abuse movement?
      a.   Controversy over spanking
      b.   Parents not receiving legal protections in Child Protective Service investigations
      c.   Family relationship may be harmed
      d.   Lack of reporting of abuse

8.   Jim frequently refers to his daughter as "stupid" or "dumb." This might be considered
      a.   Neglect
      b.   Sexual abuse
      c.   Emotional abuse
      d.   Physical abuse

9.   In Europe, possible reasons for *charavari* included
      a.   Committing adultery
      b.   Women being unemployed or failing to work
      c.   Men beating their wives
      d.   Both (a) and (b)

10. The shelter movement was started primarily by
     a. Former batterers who felt guilty
     b. Feminist groups and organization
     c. Men wanting to protect women
     d. Members of the U.S. Congress

11. John has just purchased roses for his wife because of a very violent fight they had the evening before. This behavior would fall into which part of Walker's cycle of violence?
     a. Tension building
     b. Explosion
     c. Crises
     d. Loving and contrite

12. The concept that has been often used in legal cases from Walker's model is
     a. The battered woman syndrome
     b. Learned helplessness
     c. Vigilante justice
     d. Both (a) and (b)

13. A debate about mandatory arrest of batterers might be an indicator of
     a. The "male-perpetrator" oriented phase
     b. Fragmentation of the spouse-abuse movement
     c. Traditional inertia
     d. Ironic deconstruction

14. Mutual spousal abuse or the "Saturday night brawler" script would be an example of
     a. Fragmentation of the spousal abuse movement
     b. Illustration of systemic approach
     c. Changing gender roles
     d. All of the above

15. Which of the following is not one of the types of violence Johnson discusses?
     a. Intimate terrorism
     b. Patriarchal terrorism
     c. Common couple violence
     d. Violent restraint

16. Which of the following was not discussed as a correlate of family violence?
     a. Race
     b. Social isolation
     c. Intergenerational patterns of violence
     d. Religious denomination

17.   As measured by the Conflict Tactics Scale, about what percent of cases of spouse abuse are ones in which both partners were violent?
        a.   5%
        b.   10%
        c.   50%
        d.   90%

18.   The theory most likely associated with the intergenerational transmission of violence concept would be
        a.   Resource theory
        b.   Social exchange theory
        c.   Social learning theory
        d.   Symbolic interactionism

19.   Which of the following is not one of the findings of Gelles about why women might stay in abusive relationships?
        a.   If she loves her husband and wants to maintain the family
        b.   If the violence is infrequent and not severe
        c.   If she herself experienced violence as a child
        d.   If she has few resources

20.   The idea that a battered spouse is "sick" and can be cured would be consistent with
        a.   Individual counseling using a medical model
        b.   Family counseling using a systemic perspective
        c.   Individual counseling using a behavioral approach
        d.   Family counseling using a feminist approach

True/False

1.   Families before the Great Depression tended to handle problems with less external assistance than do today's families.
2.   In terms of producing conflict, the top-ranking issue for most couples is sex.
3.   Social movements are more successful if they demonstrate that there are deserving victims.
4.   Prior to the child-abuse movement, situations of family violence were generally handled as "family matters."
5.   Most sexual abuse involves penetration of a vagina by a penis.
6.   In the National Family Violence Surveys, over half of the respondents with children said they had slapped or spanked their child in the past year.
7.   The shelter movement experienced its largest growth in the 1970s.
8.   Mandatory arrest has been the best solution for family violence.
9.   Married people are more likely to be victims of violence than single people.
10. Few studies have found evidence of violence in same-sex relationships.

Matching

The terms introduced in this chapter are listed here in alphabetical order. Match the terms with the appropriate definition.

____	1	Charavari	A	Seeing and judging the past or future using today's definitions.
____	2	Child abuse	B	A large number of persons who join together to bring about or resist some social or cultural change.
____	3	Child neglect	C	A noisy public demonstration to subject wayward individuals to humiliation in the eyes of the community.
____	4	Claims maker	D	Action by a parent or parent surrogate that should not have been done because of potential harm to the child.
____	5	Coping	E	Events with the potential of causing major change in a family system.
____	6	Crisis	F	Failure of a parent or parent surrogate to do something they should have done for their child.
____	7	Moral entrepreneurs	G	Management of stressors without detrimental effects to the family system.
____	8	Presentism	H	People who risk moral capital to produce social change.
____	9	Social movement	I	Person who puts forth a particular view of reality in support of, or in response to, a social movement.
____	10	Stressors	J	The period of disorganization resulting from a stressor that ordinary coping mechanism have trouble dealing with.

Short Essay

1. Explain the following scenario using Hill's or McCubbin's models of family stress. Be sure to identify each component clearly. Joshua and Tiffany have recently been married and just found out that she is pregnant with their first child. Tiffany had been working part time at a food warehouse and Joshua was working with a construction crew but looking for a better position. Tiffany's uncle just told them about a friend of his who was opening a new business that Joshua would be perfect for, at a substantial bonus. The drawback is they must move 200 miles away from their extended family. Joshua has begun "going out with the guys" after work because he says he is feeling "stressed" by so many decisions.
2. Discuss some of the research issues and concerns when studying family violence. Use the shelter movement and the Conflict Tactics Scale and examples to support your points.

Critical Thinking

1. Investigate some of the ways in which domestic violence may differ between heterosexual and same sex couples. Good places to begin include (http://www.lambda.org/DV_background.htm) and (http://www.psychpage.com/learning/library/gay/gayviol.html).
2. Find out what the local statistics are for your area concerning child abuse and family violence. You might begin by investigating the links at (http://www.jimhopper.com/abstats/) or (http://www.os.dhhs.gov/news/press//2001pres/20010402.html).
3. The U.S. Department of Justice houses the Department of Violence Against Women (http://www.usdoj.gov/ovw/), which, among other things, enforces the Violence Against Women Act. Using theoretical perspectives and data from this chapter, elsewhere in the textbook, and outside sources, answer the following question: Why is there no government Department of Violence Against Men?

Additional Small Group Discussions

Consider the following possible policy changes regarding child abuse:
> 1. Exposing children to second-hand tobacco smoke should be considered child abuse.
> 2. Spanking should be considered child abuse.

How does your group feel about these possible changes? What would happen to the rate of child abuse if either change was adopted?

Select one of these changes and consider the following: Suppose you felt very strongly about one of these issues and want to create social change to get the policy adopted by your state legislature. Considering "social movement theory," how would you go about getting the change made?

Answer Keys

Multiple Choice

1.	b	6.	c	11.	d	16.	d
2.	d	7.	d	12.	d	17.	c
3.	d	8.	c	13.	b	18.	d
4.	c	9.	d	14.	b	19.	a
5.	d	10.	b	15.	d	20.	a

True/False

1.	t		6.	t
2.	f		7.	t
3.	t		8.	f
4.	t		9.	f
5.	f		10.	f

Matching

1.	C		6.	J
2.	D		7.	H
3.	F		8.	A
4.	I		9.	B
5.	G		10.	E

Short Essay

1. Explain the following scenario using Hill's or McCubbin's models of family stress. Be sure to identify each component clearly. Joshua and Tiffany have recently been married and just found out that she is pregnant with their first child. Tiffany had been working part time at a food warehouse and Joshua was working with a construction crew but looking for a better position. Tiffany's uncle just told them about a friend of his who was opening a new business that Joshua would be perfect for, at a substantial bonus. The drawback is they must move 200 miles away from their extended family. Joshua has begun "going out with the guys" after work because he says he is feeling "stressed" by so many decisions.
    a. A = new job opportunity and pregnancy
    b. B = are employed, have extended family support
    c. C = young, not married long, financial strains
    d. X = (what A, B, and C might make X a crisis)?

2. Discuss some of the research issues and concerns when studying family violence. Use the shelter movement and the Conflict Tactics Scale and examples to support your points.
    a. Issues of measurement and definition of violence—refer to Johnson study
    b. Differing theoretical perspectives
    c. Truthfulness in responses on self-report studies and anecdotal studies
    d. Boundary crossing of advocacy/political agenda and research

Chapter 15 Divorce and Rescripted Families

Learning Objectives

After reading this chapter, you should be able to
1. Explain how and why the divorce rate has increased with industrialization.
2. Discuss the United States as a "postdivorce" society.
3. Identify the variables associated with divorce.
4. Describe the stages of divorce.
5. Discuss the potential effects of divorce on children.
6. Describe the characteristics of stepfamilies and the likelihood for remarriages to succeed or fail.
7. Discuss the incidence and impact of remarriage and stepfamilies.
8. Explain the overall influence of divorce on society.

Chapter Outline

Thinking Ahead: What do you think has happened to the divorce rate in the United States in the last thirty years? Why? How does this compare to other countries? What kinds of social changes would be likely to lower the divorce rate? Would these changes be desirable? In what ways do stepfamilies differ from intact families? How would family systems theorists answer these questions? Feminist theorists? Scripting theorists?

1) Divorce in Comparative Context
    a)   Ending the marital union
    b)   Modes of production and divorce
         i)   Hunting-gathering divorce
         ii)   Divorce in Agrarian societies
         iii) Industrialization and divorce
    c)   Divorce in the United States
    d)   The divorce revolution
    e)   The postdivorce society
         i)   Family bonds
         ii)   Inequality
         iii) Structural and cultural factors

2) Divorce "Whys"
    a)   Macro-sociological and demographic variables
         i)   Race and ethnicity
         ii)   Socioeconomic status
         iii) Employment type
         iv) Age
         v)   Duration of marriage

        vi) Religion
        vii) Children
        viii)Other factors
   b)   Personal "whys"

3) The Divorce Process and Outcome
   a)   The stations of divorce
        i)   Emotional
        ii)   Legal
        iii) Economic
        iv) Coparental
        v)   Community
        vi) Psychic
   b)   Outcomes of divorce

4) Children of Divorce
   a)   Divorce-related stressors
   b)   Children at risk
   c)   Resilience
   d)   Distress without disorders
   e)   Diverse outcomes in children of divorce

5) Remarriage and Stepfamilies
   a)   Remarriage and cohabitation after divorce
   b)   Remarriage process and quality
   c)   Stepfamilies

Multiple Choice Questions

1.   Legal annulments are
       a.   Relatively common today
       b.   Relatively rare today
       c.   Preferred more by Protestants than by Catholics
       d.   Both (b) and (c)

2.   With industrialization, marriages begin to
       a.   Be seen more as a matter of individual development
       b.   Dissolve less rapidly than in hunter-gather societies
       c.   Become more extrinsic in nature
       d.   Both (a) and (c)

3. In the New England colonies, divorce was
    a. Common
    b. Rare but possible
    c. Unheard of
    d. Grounds for the death penalty

4. Over the last century, the highest short-term peak in the divorce rate occurred
    a. During the 1920s
    b. After the First World War
    c. After the Second World War
    d. During the Vietnam War

5. Joint legal custody is associated with
    a. Better relationships between ex-partners
    b. Better relationships between fathers and children
    c. Better relationships between mothers and children
    d. No change in relationships

6. Research suggests the strongest factor concerning whether a parent pays child support to be
    a. Ratio of total income to total financial burden
    b. Relationship status with ex-partner
    c. Current marital status
    d. None of the above

7. Which of the following is not a characteristic of a "postdivorce" society
    a. Weakening intergenerational ties
    b. Increasing number of stepfamilies
    c. Equality in standards of living between men and women
    d. Changing values concerning families and relationships

8. Which of the following statements is most true concerning macro-level correlates of divorce?
    a. The higher the level of education the higher the divorce rate
    b. The age of marriage is the strongest predictor of divorce
    c. Lowest divorce rates are found among those with no religious affiliation
    d. Couples who do shift work are not likely to divorce

9. Which of the following is correct?
    a. Divorce rates are lowest in the southeastern states
    b. Rural couples have higher divorce rates than urban couples
    c. Couples who cohabit prior to marriage are more likely to divorce
    d. Adults whose parents divorced are less likely to divorce

10.   Stephanie has been thinking about leaving Steve for several months. She has been less willing to disclose personal feelings and information and seems cold and distant. She is dealing with which of the stations of divorce?
    a.   Legal
    b.   Emotional
    c.   Coparental
    d.   Economic

11.   Which of the following is not a characteristic of divorced adults?
    a.   More health problems
    b.   Less satisfying sex lives
    c.   Better self-concepts
    d.   More social isolation

12.   Which of the following is not a divorce-related stressor for children?
    a.   Moving to a new neighborhood
    b.   Financial changes, usually downward
    c.   More conflict with both parents
    d.   All the above are stressors

13.   Children of divorce are subject to numerous risk factors; which of the following is not a major risk factor or behavior?
    a.   Incarceration and delinquent behavior
    b.   Earlier sexual activity
    c.   Drug and alcohol usage
    d.   Less social support from friends

14.   Which of the following is not an issue that children of divorce would be likely to worry about?
    a.   Parental attendance at events such as graduations
    b.   Whether or not fathers love them
    c.   Amount of time spent with fathers
    d.   Amount of time spent with friends

15.   Which of the following is not true concerning remarriage?
    a.   The younger a woman is at divorce the more likely she is to remarry
    b.   The more children a woman has custody of the more likely she is to remarry
    c.   Better educated men are more likely to remarry
    d.   Better educated women are less likely to remarry, especially if they have more than four years of college

16. Remarried spouses are
    a. More likely to openly express criticisms, anger, and irritation than first-married couples
    b. Less likely to report high levels of marital satisfaction
    c. More likely to have financial difficulties
    d. All of the above

17. Which of the following is not a characteristic of stepfamilies?
    a. Lack a shared family history
    b. Have less stress
    c. Are less cohesive
    d. Have more loyalty conflicts

18. Christine is divorced and has custody of her three children. She has recently married a man who does not have custody of his three children. On some visitation weekends there are six children in their household, other weekends there are none. It is unclear to the children which household rules to go by on which weekends. This condition of not knowing who is in the family and who is not would illustrate
    a. Remarriage chains
    b. Boundary ambiguity
    c. Role conflict
    d. None of the above

19. Which is not true concerning stepparents?
    a. Mothers in stepfamilies fare almost as well as mothers in first marriages
    b. Stepparents do not legally have to pay child support for their stepchildren
    c. Often stepparents have no legal rights to records such as school documents
    d. All of the above are true

20. Better adolescent adjustment is reported in stepparent families when the stepparent
    a. Is less active in both support and control
    b. Punishes more
    c. Is a friend to the stepchild
    d. Has little part in discipline

True/False

1. Prior to industrialization in Europe, divorces were common.
2. The tender years rule means that people should not divorce when children are young.
3. Mothers retain custody in about 90% of divorce cases.
4. In general, higher socioeconomic status is associated with lower divorce rates.
5. Jewish people have the highest divorce rates.

6.   According to a Gallup poll, the leading cause given for marital breakup was "personality differences or incompatibility."
7.   Divorce is a major cause of poverty among women and their custodial children.
8.   Divorced men and women have higher rates of psychological well-being than married couples.
9.   Many divorced women experience improvements in their careers and report higher levels of happiness than before divorce.
10. According to Wallerstein's longitudinal study, five years after the divorce, 40% of the children remained moderately or severely depressed.
11. Amato and Booth found that marital quality is related to parent-child relationships as much as twelve years before divorce actually occurs.
12. Children's adjustment is not related to the amount of parental conflict.

Matching

The terms introduced in this chapter are listed here in alphabetical order. Match the terms with the appropriate definition.

_____	1	Alimony	A	Divorce.
_____	2	Boundary ambiguity	B	Marked by an ability to recover quickly from misfortune.
_____	3	Crude divorce rate	C	A condition in which a married couple separates, has a legally recognized property and custody settlement, lives apart, but may not remarry.
_____	4	Desertion	D	A condition in which married couples maintain separate residences because of problems living together.
_____	5	Dissolution of marriage	E	A conflict-resolution process in which a third party helps a couple resolve divorce issues.
_____	6	Divorce mediation	F	Connections that link individuals across households through ties of disrupted and new unions.
_____	7	Informal separation	G	Legally or culturally unjustified abandonment of a spouse, children, or both.
_____	8	Joint custody	H	Number of divorces per year per 1,000 married women age fifteen and older
_____	9	Legal separation	I	Number of divorces per year per 1,000 persons in the population.
_____	10	Refined divorce rate	J	Support paid to a spouse by the former spouse after divorce or separation.
_____	11	Remarriage chains	K	The awarding of shared residential or legal custody to both parents after divorce.

	12	Resilient	L	The legal guideline that young children are better off living with their mothers.
	13	Tender years rule	M	Uncertainty about who is considered part of a particular family system, or what roles the members should play.

Short Essay

1. Outline Bohannon's stages of divorce model and discuss the possible uses of this typology.
2. Using Judith Wallerstein's longitudinal research, discuss some of the risk factors associated with being a child of divorced parents.

Critical Thinking

1. One possible solution for the high divorce rates utilized by several states is "covenant marriages." Investigate which states have this as an option and what it entails. Do you think this is a good idea? Why or why not?
2. Read one of the articles posted at http://www.futureofchildren.org/ (search by keyword "divorce"). Write a one-page essay discussing how this information supports or refutes what you already have learned about children and divorce.
3. One reviewer of this textbook complained because she believed the book reported too much negative research about the impact of divorce on children. Her argument was, "Many of the students will have grown up in divorced families, and the discussion of negative outcomes might make them feel bad." Respond in depth to that reviewer's criticism.

Additional Small Group Discussions

Do you think the divorce rate is too high? Why, why not? What could be done to lower the rate? Would your group support a "covenant marriage" law for your state? Why or why not?

Answer Keys

Multiple Choice

1.	b	6.	a	11.	c	16.	a
2.	a	7.	c	12.	d	17.	b
3.	b	8.	b	13.	d	18.	b
4.	c	9.	c	14.	d	19.	d
5.	b	10.	b	15.	b	20.	a

True/False

1.	f		7.	t
2.	f		8.	f
3.	t		9.	t
4.	t		10.	t
5.	t		11.	t
6.	f		12.	f

Matching

1.	J		8.	K
2.	M		9.	C
3.	I		10.	H
4.	G		11.	F
5.	A		12.	B
6.	E		13.	L
7.	D			

Short Essay

1. Outline Bohannon's stages of divorce model and discuss the possible uses of this typology.
   a. Emotional
   b. Legal
   c. Psychic
   d. Community
   e. Economic
   f. Coparental
   g. Used: to help people understand different aspects of divorce and realize not everyone will respond the same way or be in the same part of the process.

2. Using Judith Wallerstein's longitudinal research, discuss some of the risk factors associated with being a child of divorced parents.
   a. Emotional reactions of shock, shame, anger, disbelief, and grief
   b. Tendency to blame one parent or the other
   c. Depression
   d. Hope that parents would get back together
   e. Difficulty forming intimate relationships later in life

Chapter 16 Family Perspectives, Policy and the Future

Learning Objectives

After reading this chapter, you should be able to
1. Discuss the "pessimist" perspective in terms of the future of the family.
2. Describe the "glad it changed" position and contrast it to the "pessimist" position.
3. Apply several continua in a macro-sociological analysis of family change.
4. Describe a variety of roles that family researchers can play.
5. Be able to speculate about the future of the family in American and the world.

Chapter Outline

Thinking Ahead: Based on what you have learned in this course, do you agree more with the Pessimistic or Optimistic view of the future of the family? List several political issues that directly affect the family. If you were president, how would you deal with these issues?

1) Images of the Past, Present, and Future
    a) Family continua, change, and interpretations
        i) Mate selection
        ii) Gender roles
        iii) Socialization
        iv) Personnel embeddedness
        v) Institutional embeddedness

2) Other Future Considerations

3) Family Policy
    a) Family policy roles
        i) Research for family policy
        ii) Family evaluation research
        iii) Family impact analysis
        iv) Family policy advocacy
    b) Family policy issues
    c) Complexity and unintended consequences

4) The Family in Advanced Postindustrialism
    a) A scenario
    b) The author's conclusions

Rethinking in Context: Would you like to live in the kind of family depicted in the "postindustrial family" scenario? Why or why not? What kind of future do you see for the family in America and in the world?

Multiple Choice Questions

1. Change on the mate selection continuum suggests movement toward
    a. The completely controlled end
    b. Restricted choice
    c. Total choice
    d. Open choice

2. Marriage rates are
    a. Going up
    b. Going down
    c. Staying the same

3. On the gender role continuum, movement is toward
    a. Total differentiation with clear roles
    b. Androgyny with more blurred roles
    c. Exactly in the middle
    d. No change

4. The perspective that men still do not do equal amounts of housework represents the
    _____ perspective
    a. Pessimist
    b. Glad it changed
    c. It's still the same
    d. None of the above

5. The direction of change on the socialization continuum is toward
    a. Extra-familial orderly replacement
    b. Agencies, identifications problematic
    c. Redefinition of culture by each generation
    d. Stability

6. Movement on the personnel embeddedness continuum is toward
    a. Kin group basic
    b. Nuclear family basic
    c. Individual basic
    d. No change

7.   Suzanne has decided she "needs a break" from her fifteen-year marriage, so she is going on a month-long vacation by herself. This perspective would represent which perspective on the personnel embeddedness continuum?
        a.   Point A
        b.   Point B
        c.   Point C
        d.   Not represented

8.   Which of the following would "pessimists" not see as evidence of family decline?
        a.   Geographic mobility
        b.   Relative prosperity
        c.   Cultural complexity
        d.   Increase in age at marriage

9.   Pessimists might be encouraged by all the following changes except
        a.   Rates of unwed birth going down
        b.   Crime rates going down
        c.   Abortion rates going down
        d.   Teenage pregnancy rates going up

10.   Which of the following is not one of the four major roles Nye and McDonald outlined for family policy researchers?
        a.   Family evaluation
        b.   Family impact analysis
        c.   Family economic analysis
        d.   Family policy advocacy

11.   An unbiased researcher who is investigating children being raised by gay or lesbian parents would fall into the category of
        a.   Research for family policy
        b.   Family evaluation research
        c.   Family impact analysis
        d.   Family policy advocacy

12.   Researchers who look at programs such as Head Start would be doing which type of research?
        a.   Research for family policy
        b.   Family evaluation research
        c.   Family impact analysis
        d.   Family policy advocacy

13.   Which of the following is not an issue that is likely to receive much attention for family policy makers in the near future?
     a.   Same sex marriages
     b.   Rights of parents versus rights of children
     c.   Legal and moral definitions of family
     d.   All of the above are significant issues

14.   What one factor is most likely to influence the future of the family in terms of day-to-day functioning according to the scenario provided by the textbook author?
     a.   Changes in gender roles
     b.   Changes in the economy
     c.   Changes in telecommunication and technology
     d.   Changes in childrearing

True/False

1.   On the mate selection continuum, if the direction of change continues in the future, divorce rates will fall.
2.   Childbearing does not continue to have a "traditionalizing" influence on marriage.
3.   Androgyny is limited by sex-irreducible gender roles.
4.   Children being raised by institutions fall toward the extra-familial orderly replacement end of the socialization continuum.
5.   De-fathering of the family means that fathers have declining involvement in the typical socialization process of children.
6.   Personal embeddedness deals with the extent that persons in a system are part of a larger family group.
7.   Fewer Americans live by themselves today than at any other time in American history.
8.   The increasing gap between the rich and poor is especially evident in Hispanic and Black communities.
9.   The United States is considered to be behind many other industrialized nations with respect to family policy.
10. The federal government determines most marriage and divorce laws.

Short Essay

1.   Using the scenario described at the end of this chapter, provide one example from each perspective (pessimist, glad it changed, and it's still the same) and discuss how the scenario supports that viewpoint.
2.   Discuss how some types of research might fall into several components of Nye and McDonald's typology. You may select your own example or use the suggestions provided by your textbook author of researchers who investigate children being raised in gay or lesbian households.

Critical Thinking

1. Select any of the issues concerning family policy and investigate them further via the Internet or other resources. Have there been any recent political or family policy movements on your particular topic?
2. Discuss the impacts of "de-fathering" of the family. Use information you have learned about in this course to support or refute the claims you make.

Additional Small Group Discussions

Locate the contemporary United States on each of the following continua: Mate Selection, Gender Roles, Socialization, Personnel Embeddedness, and Institutional Embeddedness. Select one of these, and decide in which direction you would like to see the country move. What public policy decisions might be helpful in moving the country in the desired direction?

Answer Keys

Multiple Choice

1.	c	5.	c	9.	d	13.	d
2.	b	6.	c	10.	c	14.	c
3.	b	7.	c	11.	a		
4.	b	8.	d	12.	b		

True/False

1.	f	6.	t
2.	f	7.	f
3.	t	8.	t
4.	f	9.	t
5.	t	10.	f

Short Essay

1. Using the scenario described at the end of this chapter, provide one example from each perspective (pessimist, glad it changed, and it's still the same) and discuss how it supports that viewpoint.
    a. Pessimist—less family interaction, less work-related interaction, more social isolation leading to more breakdown of family as institution
    b. Glad it changed—more flexibility in work world, less division of gender-based household tasks, better extended family communication
    c. Still the same—family is still living in a small group unit with relationships being the primary focus of their day

2.   Discuss how some types of research might fall into several components of Nye and
     McDonald's typology. You may select your own example or use the suggestions
     provided by yout textbook author of researchers who investigate children being raised in
     gay or lesbian households.

Survey of Opinions and Experiences

Participation in this survey is voluntary. For those who choose to participate, your answers are completely anonymous. Do not put your name on this form or on the answer sheet. We will use the results of the completed surveys to generate discussion about several issues during the course. If you choose to participate, please be as honest as possible. Circle the letter that best summarizes your answer. Thank you for your contribution.

1. What is your sex?
    a. female
    b. male

2. What is your race/ethnicity/origin?
    a. Hispanic
    b. Black
    c. White
    d. Asian
    e. Other or Mixed

3. What is your current marital status?
    a. Married
    b. Widowed
    c. Divorced
    d. Separated
    e. Never Married

4. When you were fourteen, would you say your family income was below average, average, or above average?
    a. Below average
    b. Average
    c. Above average

5. While growing up, did you ever live in a single parent or step family?
    a. Yes
    b. No

6. How often do you attend religious services?
    a. At least weekly
    b. About once a month
    c. About once a year
    d. Less than once a year

7. If you were asked to use one of four names for your social class, in which would you say you belong?
   a. Lower class
   b. Working class
   c. Middle class
   d. Upper class

8. Should divorce in this country be easier or more difficult to obtain than it is now?
   a. Easier
   b. More difficult
   c. Stay as is

9. What do you think is the ideal number of children for you to have?
   a. 0
   b. 1
   c. 2
   d. 3
   e. 4 or more

10. How many children do you now have?
    a. 0
    b. 1
    c. 2
    d. 3
    e. 4 or more

11. Having children interferes too much with the freedom of parents—do you agree or disagree?
    a. Strongly agree
    b. Agree
    c. Neither
    d. Disagree
    e. Strongly disagree

12. Watching kids grow up is life's greatest joy—do you agree or disagree?
    a. Strongly agree
    b. Agree
    c. Neither agree nor disagree
    d. Disagree
    e. Strongly disagree

13. Which of these would you say is more important in preparing children for life…to be obedient or to think for themselves?
> a. To be obedient
> b. To think for themselves

14. About how often do you spend a social evening with relatives?
> a. Not often
> b. Monthly
> c. Weekly

15. It is much better for everyone involved if the man is the achiever outside the home and the woman takes care of the home and family.
> a. Strongly agree
> b. Agree
> c. Disagree
> d. Strongly disagree

16. Taken all together, how would you say things are these days? Would you say that you are very happy, pretty happy, or not too happy?
> a. Very happy
> b. Pretty happy
> c. Not too happy

17. ANSWER THIS QUESTION ONLY IF YOU ARE CURRENTLY MARRIED: Taking things all together, how would you describe your marriage? Would you say that your marriage is very happy, pretty happy, or not too happy?
> a. Very happy
> b. Pretty happy
> c. Not too happy

18. If a male and female in their early teens, say fourteen to sixteen years old, have sex relations before marriage do you think it is always wrong, almost always wrong, wrong only sometimes, or not wrong at all?
> a. Always wrong
> b. Almost always wrong
> c. Wrong only sometimes
> d. Not wrong at all

19. Is homosexuality wrong?
> a. Always wrong
> b. Almost always wrong
> c. Sometimes wrong
> d. Not at all wrong

20. Do you think being homosexual is something people choose to be, or do you think it is something they cannot change?
    a. Choose
    b. Cannot change

21. Do you think marriages between homosexuals should or should not be recognized by the law as valid, with the same rights as traditional marriages?
    a. Should
    b. Should not

22. Do you agree or disagree that it is sometimes necessary to discipline a child with a good, hard spanking?
    a. Agree
    b. Disagree

23. Families should receive financial benefits for child care when both parents work—do you agree or disagree?
    a. Strongly agree
    b. Agree
    c. Neither agree nor disagree
    d. Disagree
    e. Strongly disagree

24. How important to you is being married?
    a. One of the most important things
    b. Important
    c. Not too important

25. How important to you is having children?
    a. The most important thing
    b. Important
    c. Less important than some other things

26. Have you ever been punched or beaten by another person?
    a. Yes
    b. No

27. How close do you feel to your mother?
    a. Extremely close
    b. Quite close
    c. Fairly close
    d. Not very close

28. How close do you feel to your father?
   a. Extremely close
   b. Quite close
   c. Fairly close
   d. Not very close

29. How old were you when you began dating?
   a. 14 or less
   b. 15
   c. 16
   d. 17
   e. 18 or more

30. How old were you when you had voluntary sexual intercourse for the first time?
   a. 15 or younger
   b. 16
   c. 17
   d. 18 or over
   e. Haven't had sexual intercourse

31. (This question was omitted)

32. Was there ever a time when you were forced to have sex against your will, or raped?
   a. Yes
   b. No

33. How many of your friends have had sexual intercourse?
   a. Most
   b. Several
   c. Just a few
   d. None

34. Before you turned eighteen did you ever run away from home?
   a. Yes
   b. No

Following are six situations in which a woman might want to have an abortion. Indicate whether you think a woman should be allowed to have a legal abortion in each situation.
LEGAL ABORTION should be allowed if . . . .

35. There is a strong chance of serious defect in the baby.
   a. Yes
   b. No

36. She is married and does not want any more children.
    a. Yes
    b. No

37. The woman's own health is seriously endangered by the pregnancy.
    a. Yes
    b. No

38. The family has a very low income and cannot afford any more children.
    a. Yes
    b. No

39. She became pregnant as a result of rape.
    a. Yes
    b. No

40. She is not married and does not want to marry the man.
    a. Yes
    b. No

(END OF ABORTION QUESTIONS)

41. If you were to have a child right now, would you rather have a boy or a girl?
    a. Boy
    b. Girl

42. Are there any situations that you can imagine in which you would approve of a husband slapping his wife's face?
    a. Yes
    b. No

43. Are there any situations that you can imagine in which you would approve of a wife slapping her husband's face?
    a. Yes
    b. No

44. When you were growing up, do you remember any time when you were punched or kicked or choked by a parent or other adult guardian?
    a. Yes
    b. No

45. Do you remember ever receiving a more serious physical punishment from a parent or adult guardian than being punched, kicked, or choked?
    a. Yes
    b. No

46. What is your year in college?
    a. Freshman
    b. Sophomore
    c. Junior
    d. Senior
    e. Other

47. What is your age?
    a. 16–20
    b. 21–23
    c. 24–27
    d. 28 or over

48. Have you ever lived with a romantic partner to whom you were not then married?
    a. Yes
    b. No

49. Have you ever had a sexual experience with a person of your same sex?
    a. Yes
    b. No

50. What is the ideal age for someone of your gender to get married?
    a. under 18
    b. 18–22
    c. 23–26
    d. 27–30
    e. over 30

51. Do you think that the theory of evolution provides a good explanation about the origin of the human species?
    a. Yes
    b. No
    c. Don't know

52. What is your religious preference?
    a. Protestant
    b. Catholic
    c. Jewish
    d. Other religion
    e. No religion